# FOLLOWING THE STAR

## Daily Reflections for Advent and Christmas

Reverend Mark Boyer

**LIGUORI**
PUBLICATIONS

One Liguori Drive
Liguori, Missouri 63057
(314) 464-2500

Imprimi Potest:
William A. Nugent, C.SS.R.
Provincial, St. Louis Province
The Redemptorists

Imprimatur:
Monsignor Maurice F. Byrne
Vice Chancellor, Archdiocese of St. Louis

ISBN 0-89243-305-1
Library of Congress Catalog Card Number: 89-84465

*Dedicated to
my godchildren:
Laura Kay Pashia
and
Zachary Douglas Kinler*

# TABLE OF CONTENTS

**Introduction** . . . . . . . . . . . . . . . . . . . . . . . . . . . . . . . . . . . . . . . 9

**FIRST SUNDAY OF ADVENT**
  Cycle A: Mountains to Climb . . . . . . . . . . . . . . . . . . . . . 16
  Cycle B: Clay to Be Formed . . . . . . . . . . . . . . . . . . . . . 17
  Cycle C: Promises to Keep . . . . . . . . . . . . . . . . . . . . . 18
Monday: Swords Into Plowshares . . . . . . . . . . . . . . . . . 19
Tuesday: Line of David . . . . . . . . . . . . . . . . . . . . . . . . 21
Wednesday: Top of the Mountain . . . . . . . . . . . . . . . . . 22
Thursday: Rock of Security . . . . . . . . . . . . . . . . . . . . . 23
Friday: God's Orchard . . . . . . . . . . . . . . . . . . . . . . . . . 25
Saturday: A Listening God . . . . . . . . . . . . . . . . . . . . . 26
December 8: SOLEMNITY OF THE IMMACULATE
CONCEPTION
  Hiding From God . . . . . . . . . . . . . . . . . . . . . . . . . . . . . 27

**SECOND SUNDAY OF ADVENT**
  Cycle A: Portrait of Peace . . . . . . . . . . . . . . . . . . . . . 30
  Cycle B: Herald of Good News . . . . . . . . . . . . . . . . . . 31
  Cycle C: Dress for Glory . . . . . . . . . . . . . . . . . . . . . . 33
Monday: A Desert Experience . . . . . . . . . . . . . . . . . . . 35
Tuesday: Prepare the Way . . . . . . . . . . . . . . . . . . . . . . 37
Wednesday: Acknowledge Equality . . . . . . . . . . . . . . . 38
Thursday: Shared Power . . . . . . . . . . . . . . . . . . . . . . . 40
Friday: God, Our Teacher . . . . . . . . . . . . . . . . . . . . . . 42
Saturday: God's Fire . . . . . . . . . . . . . . . . . . . . . . . . . . 43
December 12: FEAST OF OUR LADY OF GUADALUPE
  Rejoice With Mary . . . . . . . . . . . . . . . . . . . . . . . . . . . 45

## THIRD SUNDAY OF ADVENT

Cycle A: Fear Not! ................................ 48
Cycle B: Robed in Justice ........................ 49
Cycle C: Exult in the Lord ...................... 51
Monday: Follow the Star .......................... 52
Tuesday: Faithful Remnant ........................ 54
Wednesday: God's Justice ......................... 55
Thursday: Return to God .......................... 57
Friday: Healing Divisions ........................ 59
December 17: Signs of Power ...................... 61
December 18: Promises Kept ....................... 63

## FOURTH SUNDAY OF ADVENT

Cycle A: Signs of God's Presence ................. 66
Cycle B: Temples of God .......................... 68
Cycle C: Place of Origin ......................... 69
December 19: Roots ............................... 71
December 20: Signs From God ...................... 73
December 21: God of Love (First Option)........... 75
December 21: God's Presence (Second Option) ...... 76
December 22: Dedication .......................... 78
December 23: God's Messenger ..................... 80
December 24: Greatness Comes From God (Morning)... 82
December 24: Espoused of God (Vigil of Christmas) ... 84
December 25: SOLEMNITY OF CHRISTMAS
Midnight: Night Into Day ......................... 85
Dawn: Called by Name ............................. 87
Daytime: God Is King ............................. 89
December 26: FEAST OF SAINT STEPHEN
Faithful Follower ................................ 90
December 27: FEAST OF SAINT JOHN
Proclamation ..................................... 92

December 28: FEAST OF THE HOLY INNOCENTS
Darkness and Light ............................. 94
December 29: True Christians ....................... 96
December 30: Communication ...................... 98
December 31: Final Hour .......................... 99
FEAST OF THE HOLY FAMILY
Mutual Respect ................................ 100
January 1: SOLEMNITY OF MARY, MOTHER OF GOD
Mary's Name ................................ 102
January 2: Hearing God's Word ..................... 104
January 3: Children of God ........................ 105
January 4: Truly Holy ............................ 107
January 5: Love One Another ...................... 108
January 6: Three Testifiers ........................ 110
January 7: False Gods ............................ 112
SOLEMNITY OF THE EPIPHANY
God's Glory Manifested .......................... 113
Monday After Epiphany: Testing of Spirits ............ 115
Tuesday After Epiphany: God Is Love ................ 117
Wednesday After Epiphany: Love Drives Out Fear ....... 118
Thursday After Epiphany: Love of God and Neighbor .... 120
Friday After Epiphany: Victors ..................... 122
Saturday After Epiphany: Confidence in God ........... 123
FEAST OF THE BAPTISM OF THE LORD
Victory of Justice ............................... 125
Chart ........................................... 127

# INTRODUCTION

*Following the Star* was chosen as the title for this work because it reflects not only the hope of the Wise Men in a Savior but also the contemporary purpose of the current Advent and Christmas seasons. And these in turn remind us that all of life is a journey in search of our Savior who calls each of us to follow him toward the kingdom of God.

The four weeks of Advent focus on waiting for the Second Coming of the Lord in glory while remembering his first coming in history. In this way Advent is a preparation for Christmas. But the primary emphasis is on looking forward to the Lord's final coming at the end of time. This focus is geared to awaken the believer to a recognition of the Lord's daily advents into life now in what are often referred to as grace-filled moments.

This focus of Advent is made clear in the *General Norms for the Liturgical Year and The Calendar* issued in 1975 by the Sacred Congregation of Rites: "Advent has a twofold character: as a season to prepare for Christmas when Christ's first coming to us is remembered; as a season when that remembrance directs the mind and heart to await Christ's Second Coming at the end of time. Advent is thus a period for devout and joyful expectation" (#39).

During this season the believer is urged to look forward joyfully to the Second Coming of Christ while reflecting on his birth into history, his manifestation through various experiences in the lives of believers, and the Word of God proclaimed daily in the Church. At the same time the believer is drawn naturally to contemplate what are called the Last Things (death, judgment, heaven, hell).

The Lectionary for Mass provides the fare of the Word of God during Advent. In reference to Advent, the Sacred Congregation for the Sacraments and Divine Worship revised the Lectionary for Mass in 1981: "The Old Testament readings are prophecies about the Messiah and the Messianic age, especially from Isaiah" (#93). "In the first part of Advent there are readings from Isaiah, distributed in accord with the sequence of the book itself and including salient texts that are also read on the Sundays. On Thursday of the second week . . . the first reading is either a continuation of Isaiah or a text chosen in view of the gospel [about John the Baptizer]. In the last week before Christmas . . . the first reading, chosen in view of the gospel reading, [is] from different Old Testament books and includes important Messianic prophecies" (#94).

Isaiah is considered the greatest of the prophets, and his writings deserve to be one of the principal sources of reflection during Advent. The prophet offers hope in the midst of tragedy, despair, and destruction. He can foresee the day of a new city, new life, a new covenant, and the renewed presence of God. Isaiah exhorts all to remain faithful to the Lord and to watch, wait, and expect his coming in order to share fully in his approaching kingdom. There is no reason to live in fear, the prophet proclaims. The best approach is to long for the new era, to hunger for it, to remain joyful, and to rejoice in the daily coming of the Lord into everyday life.

The two to three weeks of the Christmas season are a celebration of the inauguration of the reign of God in the world today. They begin with a reflection on Jesus' manifestation in the flesh at his birth and then turn to the multiple epiphanies as he was revealed to the Gentiles. The season culminates with the account of the theophany at his baptism in the Jordan River. "Next to the yearly celebration of the paschal mystery, the Church holds most sacred the memorial of Christ's birth and early manifestations. This is the purpose of the Christmas season" (#32, *General Norms for the Liturgical Year and the Calendar*).

For the major celebrations of the Christmas season, the Vigil of Christmas, Christmas (Midnight, Dawn, and Daytime), Epiphany, and the Baptism of the Lord, the first reading is chosen from the prophet Isaiah. It is only proper that the prophet who accompanied people through the joyful expectation of Advent should find his words fulfilled in the celebrations of Christmas.

However, the Lectionary for Mass quickly moves away from the Old Testament and to the New Testament with readings from the First Letter of John. "From 29 December on, there is a continuous reading of the whole of 1 John, which actually begins earlier, on 27 December, feast of Saint John the Evangelist, and on 28 December, feast of the Holy Innocents" (#96).

The three principal feasts of Saint Stephen, Saint John, and the Holy Innocents, which follow Christmas day, illustrate what happens to those who live and travel the way of the kingdom of God while they wait for the Lord to come again in glory.

As has been seen, both the Advent season and the Christmas season have their own special focus. However, they must be taken together because they overlap like folds in a single garment. The four weeks of Advent prepare for the celebration of two to three weeks of Christmas. Together the themes of both seasons are like a multifaceted diamond splitting light and beaming it in various directions and angles.

The color of violet sparkles during Advent. This is not the deep purple of Lent; rather it is like the early morning December sunrise where the clouds on the horizon are streaked with soft, billowy violet light. The growing shortness of the daylight during December also adds to the hope and expectation of the coming of the Lord of light into the world.

In the midst of the deep winter darkness, Christmas suddenly emerges with its bright, twinkling lights on clear, crisp, cold nights and lengthening sunny days. The violet expectation of the coming of the Lord is fulfilled in the white manifestation of the kingdom of God. However, the year quickly turns and once again points the believer toward the Lord's Second Coming in glory.

The seasons of Advent and Christmas are intensifications of expectation of the Second Coming of the Lord much as a camera lens is focused on one scene out of the whole world of action and possibilities. The preparation of Advent and the realization of Christmas are meant to be an important part of the life of the believer throughout the whole year. No one knows the day or the time of the Lord's coming. Watchfulness is a characteristic of an authentic Christian life. Therefore, these two seasons are given every year to rekindle the fire of expectation and provide fuel to keep it flickering till the liturgical year brings one back to the beginning of the next Advent.

All of this eschatological expectation is easily overshadowed and lost sight of and forgotten in the secular realm. Advent, if one can call it such, begins in October with the first aisles of shelves with red and green decorations. The economic countdown begins with just so many days left in the shopping season. Not only the Advent season but the Christmas season as well ends on Christmas Eve with the computer record of the last sale of the day.

There is no Christmas season in the secular world. The day after Christmas the trees are lined up along sidewalks for trash collectors, half-price sales reign supreme, and January white sales begin. Valentine hearts appear everywhere.

What is needed is a religious revival of these precious seasons. The original intent has been lost, forgotten, or smothered by the kingdom of consumerism. It is hoped that this book might help foster a return to the expectation of Advent and to help lengthen and sustain the joy of the whole of the Christmas season.

This book may be used by individuals for private reflection and prayer and by homilists for public liturgical preaching and prayer. A four-part exercise is offered for every day of the Advent and Christmas seasons.

1. A few short verses of Scripture are taken from the first reading provided in the Lectionary for the Mass of each day. Furthermore, the days are marked with specific dates so that when a particular day is omitted a reference is made to the specific day that takes its place.

2. A reflection follows the Scripture selection. The reflection is an attempt to expand an idea or an image found in the verses from the Scripture; it can be used as the starter for a homily or it can easily be considered as a homilette in itself.

3. The reflection is followed by a question for personal meditation. The question functions as a guide for further development of the idea or image chosen in the reflection. The homilist can use the question to develop a homily or pose it to the congregation for its reflection.

4. A prayer summarizes the original theme of the Scripture reading, which was expanded in the reflection and which served as the basis for meditation. The prayer concludes the daily exercise for the individual or it can be used as a fitting conclusion to the general intercessions and the liturgy of the Word during the celebration of the Eucharist.

A devout observance of Advent and Christmas can make the difference and awaken a longing of constant joyful expectation of the Lord's coming in glory. It should be remembered that every time the community gathers for the celebration of the Eucharist, it is reminded of its watching and waiting stance for the Lord's Second Coming in glory. After the Our Father the presider prays, "Deliver us, Lord, from every evil, and grant us peace in our day. In your mercy keep us free from sin and protect us from all anxiety as we wait in joyful hope for the coming of our Savior, Jesus Christ" *(The Order of Mass)*.

Mark G. Boyer

## Using This Book

The number of days in the Advent and Christmas seasons is different from year to year. For this reason, a chart is provided on pages 127-128. Please refer to it for each day's reflection.

# First
# Sunday
# of
# Advent

## Cycle A
## Mountains to Climb

In days to come,
The mountain of the LORD's house
    shall be established as the highest mountain
    and raised above the hills.
All nations shall stream toward it.

                                        (Isaiah 2:2)

*Scripture:* Isaiah 2:1-5; Romans 13:11-14; Matthew 24:37-44

*Reflection:* Mountains are places of mystery; they draw people to themselves. The snow-capped sentinels invite people to climb or to hike or to just look and observe.

The Israelites, like other peoples, believed that their God lived on a mountain. Therefore, Isaiah can state that the "mountain of the Lord's house shall be established as the highest mountain."

The Lord is God. And so important is this Lord that "all nations" come as a steady-flowing mountain stream to him. The Lord God instructs, judges, and eliminates the weapons of war among the nations.

Today we seek peak experiences of God not only on mountains but on the ocean, near the shore, in forests, in meadows, and in many other places. Many have come to understand that the whole world is God's kingdom within which we live and have our being.

*Meditation:* In what ways are you drawn into the Lord's kingdom? Where do you find God's presence?

*Prayer:* God of the mountain, you call all nations to come to you for instruction that you may judge with justice and eliminate the weapons of war. Help us to walk in your paths. Guide us to your light and lead us to the mountain of your presence as we await the coming in glory of Jesus, your Son, who is Lord for ever and ever. Amen.

## Cycle B
## Clay to Be Formed

O LORD . . .
    we are the clay and you the potter:
    we are all the work of your hands.
                (Isaiah 64:7)

*Scripture:* Isaiah 63:16-17,19, 64:2-7; 1 Corinthians 1:3-9; Mark 13:33-37

*Reflection:* A potter takes clay and shapes it. He molds the clay into the image, the idea, that exists only in his own mind. Patiently, carefully, lovingly, the potter's gentle yet firm fingers give birth to something new.

The clay must trust the potter. The clay suffers as it takes shape, as it is stretched, as it is molded. In the process of becoming, it may have to be beaten down and molded again.

Advent is a season of remolding. God is the master potter who can mold us into patiently waiting creations. God acts in his good time. We the clay must trust that God will act and then be willing to suffer the necessary changes.

*Meditation:* In your life, what needs remolding?

*Prayer:* Potter God, out of the clay of the earth you molded man and woman, the crown of your creation, and you breathed into them the breath of life. Fill us with the same breath of spirit and shape us into the image of your Son, Jesus, whose coming in glory we await. Jesus is Lord for ever and ever. Amen.

## Cycle C
## Promises to Keep

The days are coming, says the LORD, when I will fulfill the promise I made to the house of Israel and Judah.

(Jeremiah 33:14)

*Scripture:* Jeremiah 33:14-16; 1 Thessalonians 3:12–4:2; Luke 21:25-28,34-36

*Reflection:* People make promises every day. A teenage girl promises her best friend that she will tell no one their secret. A little boy promises his mother that he will never be bad again. Adults promise each other that they will not be late. One person promises to do a favor for another.

How often these promises are broken — sometimes unintentionally, certainly not maliciously, but broken nevertheless.

We human beings are not always able to keep the promises we make. God, however, never breaks a promise. He reiterates his promises throughout time by means of prophets. He continues to send just shoots — those who do what is right and just — in order to remind us of his promises, which are yet to be kept. It is in us that God works justice, which prepares the way for his promises to become reality.

*Meditation:* What promise has the Lord made to you and kept?

*Prayer:* God of promises, you raised up Jesus, your Son, as a just shoot for David. Jesus did what was right and just. As we prepare for his coming in glory, do your work of justice through us. Keep us faithful and eliminate our slothfulness. Make us increase and overflow with love for all your people. We pray in the name of the One whose coming we await, Jesus Christ, who is Lord for ever and ever. Amen.

# Monday
## Swords Into Plowshares

They shall beat their swords into plowshares
    and their spears into pruning hooks;
One nation shall not raise the sword against another,
    nor shall they train for war again.

(Isaiah 2:4)

*Scripture:* Isaiah 4:2-6; Matthew 8:5-11

*Reflection:* Plowshares and pruning hooks are instruments of agriculture. Plowshares are used to cultivate the earth — to break its furrows, to crumble its clods, allowing the rain and oxygen to sink in. They prepare the field for planting.

Pruning hooks are used after the planting and during the growing. They cut off excess growth for the good of the whole plant. They prune so that the harvest will be bountiful.

Swords and spears are instruments of war. These cultivate defense, aggression, and, ultimately, death. Swords and spears break open people; these instruments end lives and, therefore, human dignity; they spill blood on the earth.

Today, spiritually speaking, we have many gardening tools available: friendship, healing of enmities, help for the poor, counseling centers, to name a few. All of these foster growth.

We also have war tools available: anger, hatred, gossip, racism, abortion, to name only a few. All of these foster death.

*Meditation:* Do you own more gardening tools or more war tools?

*Prayer:* God of plowshares and pruning hooks, you judge between nations and you impose your terms on many peoples. Help us to walk in your light that we may stream toward your house and turn the weapons of war into the weapons of growth. Hear our prayer as we await the coming in glory of our Lord Jesus Christ, who lives and reigns with you and the Holy Spirit, one God, for ever and ever. Amen.

## Tuesday
## Line of David

A shoot shall sprout from the stump of Jesse,
and from his roots a bud shall blossom.
(Isaiah 11:1)

*Scripture:* Isaiah 11:1-10; Luke 10:21-24

*Reflection:* The shoot sprouting from the stump of Jesse is used by the prophet Isaiah to describe a family lineage. In creating family history, many people use an outline of a tree. Great-great grandparents are found near the roots; great grandparents form the first large branches. Out on the limbs are grandparents, parents, children, and childrens' children. Such a family tree elicits a sense of belonging, of being rooted in the past.

Jesse was the stump of the Davidic family tree. From Jesse a shoot would sprout and blossom, and so it was that David was anointed as king of Israel. In the years after David's death, he became the archetype of the awaited One, the One who would deliver the people from their enemies and restore the kingdom of David.

This One would restore a sense of being rooted in the past; and we all would belong to this family tree.

*Meditation:* What gives you a sense of belonging?

*Prayer:* God of every family, from the stump of Jesse you began the royal line of David. From David's line was born your Son, a member of the human family. Root us in the hope of justice. Pour

out your Spirit on us as we await the coming in glory of our Lord
Jesus Christ, who lives and reigns with you and the Holy Spirit,
one God, for ever and ever. Amen.

# Wednesday
# Top of the Mountain

On this mountain the LORD of hosts
    will provide for all peoples
A feast of rich food and choice wines,
    juicy, rich food and pure, choice wines.
The hand of the LORD will rest on this mountain. . . .
                            (Isaiah 25:6,10)

*Scripture:* Isaiah 25:6-10; Matthew 15:29-37

*Reflection:* The Israelites believed that their God lived on the top of
a mountain. At first this may seem like an unlikely place for God to
live and to be present. However, all other ancient peoples believed
that their gods lived on mountains.

    A person needs only climb to fourteen thousand feet — even less
will do — to experience the terrible quiet of a mountain. It was on a
mountain that Elijah heard a tiny whispering sound. It was on a
mountain that Moses discovered God, worshiped God, received
the Law, and made a covenant. Jerusalem's temple was on Mount
Zion. And many other important Old Testament events took place
on mountaintops. The mountain was a sign of God's presence with
God's people.

Mountains surround us on every side — the Rockies and the Appalachians — to remind us of God's presence today. But other mountains can be signs as well. Everyday problems, messy divorces, crippling old age, cancer, AIDS, psychological instability — these are some of our personal mountains. When these are climbed, God's presence is discovered.

Any mountain is a sign that God does not abandon us. God is always with us. On whatever mountain God is found, his presence is a feast for the climber.

*Meditation:* What mountain have you most recently climbed? Did you discover God's presence there?

*Prayer:* God of the mountain, you showed your face to Moses on a summit and delivered your decalogue there. In the awful silence, Elijah heard your word and followed your will. Be with us as we climb daily. On the mountaintop let us discover the banquet of your presence and feast on the food of your grace as we await the coming in glory of your Son, our Lord Jesus Christ, who lives and reigns with you and the Holy Spirit, one God, for ever and ever. Amen.

# Thursday
# Rock of Security

Trust in the LORD forever!
For the LORD is an eternal Rock.
(Isaiah 26:4)

*Scripture:* Isaiah 26:1-6; Matthew 7:21,24-27

*Reflection:* Is the Lord an eternal rock literally or poetically? Literally, of course, the Lord is not a rock. Poetically, however, the Lord is like a rock.

Poetically a rock represents security, unchanging stability, solidity, firmness, strength. One of the older Prudential Life Insurance commercials urged people to "get a piece of the rock." Sylvester Stallone in his movie portrayal of "Rocky" also comes across "solid as a rock."

Because Isaiah views God as a rock, he is worthy of trust. Security enables people to move outward, while fear keeps them closed in and protected. People of faith profess belief in the sureness of God no matter what comes their way.

Nothing, no person, not even we ourselves, can ever foster trust like the Lord can. Things, persons, and self can be signs of security for us, but there is no security that is as steady and worthy of trust like the Lord, the Rock.

*Meditation:* Who or what stands as a sign of your security, trust, and belief that are found in God, the Rock?

*Prayer:* Eternal Rock, you live forever. Deepen our trust in you; make our footsteps sure. Humble those in high places that they might cast their eyes on the needy and the poor. Make us secure as we await the coming of your Son, Jesus, in glory. He is Lord for ever and ever. Amen.

# Friday
# God's Orchard

A very little while,
   and Lebanon shall be changed into an orchard,
and the orchard be regarded as a forest!

(Isaiah 29:17)

*Scripture:* Isaiah 29:17-24; Matthew 9:27-31

*Reflection:* An orchard is a place of growth, life, and fruit. A forest of trees blossom, leaf, and grow heavy with fresh produce. The fruit takes shape through three seasons.

In the spring the blossoms appear. During the summer the green growth thickens. In autumn the fruit ripens and is ready for the harvest.

For Isaiah, the ripened fruit was a sign for the blind, joy for the lowly, rejoicing for the poor, and the elimination of the tyrant, the arrogant, and the evildoer.

Everyone can learn a lesson from an orchard. There is always a new spring to life. Blossoming takes place and a new world suddenly unfolds ready for exploring. Maturation, deeper understanding of self, others, and God takes place during the summer of human life. Then, when autumn arrives, the first fruit, ripened by experience, can be picked. The cycle is now complete.

The fruit-laden orchard is all part of cyclically growing into the kingdom, which Jesus preached. Jesus is the ripened fruit of God's orchard; we Christians feast on that fruit.

*Meditation:* Is your orchard growing?

*Prayer:* God of the orchard, in the past you planted your people in the Promised Land, where they blossomed and grew into your special possession. From them you brought forth the ripened fruit of your Son, Jesus. Help us to produce abundantly as we await his coming again in glory, for he is Lord for ever and ever. Amen.

# Saturday
## A Listening God

[The Lord] will be gracious to you when you cry out,
as soon as he hears he will answer you.

(Isaiah 30:19)

*Scripture:* Isaiah 30:19-21,23-26; Matthew 9:35–10:1,6-8

*Reflection:* Most people are invaded and bombarded by sound and noise all day long. This severely interferes with authentic hearing or listening. When people are immersed in television, radio, stereos, elevator music, and traffic, they cannot hear what others have to say to them — especially those who may be crying out to be heard.

According to Isaiah, all the Lord does is wait to hear the cries of people. God always hears. He always answers — not in the way that people plan, but according to God's own will.

When prayers are answered, when God has heard us, or when we have really listened to others, bread has been shared. Authentic listening is like sharing bread with the hungry or sharing drink with the thirsty. Hearing an answer sound in our ears fills us with the desire to follow in the way of the One who was able to listen.

*Meditation:* Most recently, what word have you heard the Lord speak to you?

*Prayer:* God of all answers, you are gracious when we cry out, and, as soon as you hear us, you answer. Through all the noise of the world our voices sound in your ears. Enable us to hear your word in every sound of our world. Teach us to walk in your way as we wait in joyful hope for the coming in glory of your Son, Jesus Christ, who is Lord for ever and ever. Amen.

## December 8
## SOLEMNITY OF THE
## IMMACULATE CONCEPTION
### Hiding From God

"I heard you in the garden; but I was afraid, because I was naked, so I hid myself."

(Genesis 3:10)

*Scripture:* Genesis 3:9,15-20; Ephesians 1:3-6,11-12; Luke 1:26-38

*Reflection:* A garden is a place of flowers, vegetables, fruit. It is a place of delight, where God walks with people.

A person may feel earthlike in a garden, becoming all that grows there. Eden's first man and woman were naked but did not realize it until they discovered sin. Once that happened, neither of them could any longer stand unashamed before God; they felt they had to hide. They could not let God see their weakness, their vulnerability. The irony is that God had already seen their naked condition; he had created them in their nakedness and declared them "very good."

In the course of time, God created an individual to stand unashamed before God. In stark simplicity Mary stood in a garden at one with him, saying "Yes" to God's will. God prepared her, as anyone prepares a garden, for the moment when new life would begin to take root and grow in her.

Mary did not fear. She had no reason to hide. From her womb came forth the Son who was sent to lead us all back to the pristine garden so that we might live by eating the fruit of the tree of life. The Son has enabled all of us to stand before God face-to-face in our barren condition without feeling afraid, without running away to hide.

*Meditation:* What do you do when you are tempted to hide from the face of God?

*Prayer:* God of the garden, in your love you created men and women and you walk with them throughout their lives — calling them, seeking them when they hide, and wanting them to stand in plain view before you in order to receive your abundant gifts of life. Walk with us as you did with Mary. From us, bring forth good works. Enable us to see your face as we wait in joyful hope for the coming in glory of Jesus, your Son, who is Lord for ever and ever. Amen.

# Second
# Sunday
# of
# Advent

## Cycle A
## Portrait of Peace

The wolf shall be a guest of the lamb,
  and the leopard shall lie down with the kid;
The calf and the young lion shall browse together,
  with a little child to guide them.
The cow and the bear shall be neighbors,
  together their young shall rest;
  the lion shall eat hay like the ox.
The baby shall play by the cobra's den,
  and the child lay his hand on the adder's lair.
There shall be no harm or ruin on all my holy
  mountain. . . .

                              (Isaiah 11:6-9)

*Scripture:* Isaiah 11:1-10; Romans 15:4-9; Matthew 3:1-12

*Reflection:* The wallpaper in a nursery frequently has all kinds of animals printed on it. Books of children's stories often picture lambs, leopards, and kids. All of these animals, most of them natural enemies by birth, will coexist in peace, according to Isaiah's prediction.

Such is the radical quality of Isaiah's vision. With this animal imagery, he painted a picture of hope for the Israelites. Some day a descendant from Jesse's family tree would bring about a world of peace — a place that would eliminate all harm and ruin. A little child, who has no natural enemy but is trusting toward all, who is very vulnerable, would lead the world into this nursery-room picture of peace.

Oftentimes people act like the animals described by Isaiah — as if they were natural enemies of one another. One person sees himself or herself as the lamb and another person as the wolf, who is waiting for the opportunity to spring into action. One individual views herself or himself as the calf and another as the lion, who stealthily searches for someone to devour.

If we consider the equality of every person and the dignity of every person before all else, justice can be worn as a sash, faithfulness can be worn as a belt, and so-called enemies can coexist in peace. We all can arrive at such a peace — once the picture of natural enemies is changed to Isaiah's portrait of peace.

*Meditation:* What animals of conflict do you find in your life? Where is there room for potential peace?

*Prayer:* God of peace, you make enemies guests so that those in conflict lie down together, those in disagreement browse together, and those in the midst of a quarrel become neighbors. You make your people like little children, who have no natural enemies. Let your spirit rest upon us: the spirit of wisdom and understanding, the spirit of counsel and strength, the spirit of knowledge and fear of the Lord. May we see the blossoming of peace in our day as we wait for the coming in glory of the shoot from the stump of Jesse, your Son, Jesus Christ, who is Lord for ever and ever. Amen.

## Cycle B
## Herald of Good News

Go up onto a high mountain,
   Zion, herald of glad tidings;

Cry out at the top of your voice,
   Jerusalem, herald of good news!
Fear not to cry out
   and say to the cities of Judah:
Here is your God!
Here comes with power
   the LORD God. . . .
                           (Isaiah 40:9-10)

*Scripture:* Isaiah 40:1-5,9-11; 2 Peter 3:8-14; Mark 1:1-8

*Reflection:* A herald is one who delivers a message. Today there are few such heralds left. Messengers have been replaced by computers, telegrams, telephones, television, and radio. And most of the time these herald bad news instead of good news.

In ancient times the herald came running and screaming and shouting with the good news of a victory won by the army. The city waited for the herald to arrive and tell the people that their army had defeated the enemy.

What is the good news of Advent? What is the herald shouting? "Here is your God! Here comes with power the Lord God!"

In every celebration of the Eucharist this announcement is proclaimed. The presider states that all present "wait in joyful hope for the coming of our Savior, Jesus Christ." The question is this: Does anyone wait for the coming of our Lord and Savior? Phrased another way, the question is: Does anyone expect a herald to come announcing that the Lord is coming?

Our life should be a witness to this expectation. Our lifestyle should herald the Lord's coming again in glory. Advent is a liturgical season that looks into the infinite future; those who know its message understand that there is more to come. We should be the people who are heralds, messengers who are roused enough to climb high up the mountain and shout out the announcement, "Here comes the Lord God!" so that the whole world hears it.

*Meditation:* When was the last time that you were a herald of good news?

*Prayer:* Lord God, like a shepherd you feed your flock and gather the lambs in your arms, carrying them near your breast and leading the ewes with care. In the desert of our lives prepare our way. Fill in our valleys of depression and level our mountains of pride that we might herald the coming in glory of your Son, our Lord Jesus Christ, who lives and reigns with you and the Holy Spirit, one God, for ever and ever. Amen.

## Cycle C
## Dress for Glory

Jerusalem, take off your robe of mourning and misery;
    put on the splendor of glory from God forever:
Wrapped in the cloak of justice from God,
    bear on your head the mitre
that displays the glory of the eternal name.
                                                    (Baruch 5:1-2)

*Scripture:* Baruch 5:1-9; Philippians 1:4-6,8-11; Luke 3:1-6

*Reflection:* "Get dressed and let's go" is heard often when people are preparing for a wedding, a party, a dance, or a funeral. "Get dressed" means to put on the appropriate clothes, jewelry, shoes, hat, perfume, suit, tie, whatever. "Let's go" means it is time to leave the house, catch the bus, flag a cab, or get into the car and drive.

"Get dressed and let's go" is what the prophet Baruch portrays God as saying to the Israelites in Babylonian captivity. "Get dressed" means that the Israelites should put on the robe of splendor and glory. In royal clothes they should wear the cloak of justice. On their heads the miter that displays the eternal name of God is to be worn. Then, in such attire, they can take their place on the royal throne.

"Let's go" means that it is time for the Israelites to start moving, as Baruch further indicates. He tells them (in 5:5):
"Stand upon the heights;
 look to the east and see your children
Gathered from the east and the west
 at the word of the Holy One,
 rejoicing that they are remembered by God."
And he reminds them (in 5:9) that God is leading them "in joy by the light of his glory, with his mercy and justice for company."

Advent is a time for all of us to dress ourselves in justice, mercy, peace, and worship. It is a time to go and display this wondrous wardrobe, which comes from God, to the whole world.

*Meditation:* How well do you wear justice, mercy, peace, and worship of God in your daily world?

*Prayer:* God of glory, you robe your people in justice and cloak them with peace. On our heads you give us your name to bear as you trace the sign of the cross of your Son. Help us to worship your glory. Raise us up to your heights. Gather your people from east and west, Holy One, and do not forget us. Lead us in joy by the light of your glory as we advance toward the day of the Second Coming of Jesus, who is Lord for ever and ever. Amen.

## Monday
## A Desert Experience

The desert and the parched land will exult;
    the steppe will rejoice and bloom.
They will bloom with abundant flowers,
    and rejoice with joyful song.
Streams will burst forth in the desert,
    and rivers in the steppe.
The burning sands will become pools,
    and the thirsty ground, springs of water. . . .
             (Isaiah 35:1-2,6-7)

*Scripture:* Isaiah 35:1-10; Luke 5:17-26

*Reflection:* The desert usually stimulates thoughts of death. It is a place of sand, hot scorching sun, few trees, little water, and a few plants that have adapted to the heat and immediately bloom after a shower only to wither in an hour or two.

In the desert, however, there are no distractions. When Moses led the Israelites out of Egypt, they spent forty years (the number *forty* designates a long time) in the desert. Moses took the people to the desert, where they would die to their old ways, where God could speak to their hearts and form them into his people. The desert, then, is a place of formation, change, conversion. Indeed, adaptability is necessary for survival in the desert.

Isaiah sees God doing the same thing again for the Israelites, who are captive in Babylon. God will form them into the people that God wants. This is why the parched land exults, the steppe rejoices and blooms, the streams and rivers burst forth, the sands become pools, and springs rise up from baked, cracked clay.

God builds a highway, a holy way through the desert. He lures us to the desert in order to mold us in God's ways. Such deserts need not be thought of as only physical places. Other deserts exist; these include a retreat, an empty church, a prayer corner, or a weekend camping trip along a lake, complete with a tent. A true desert experience can bring about many changes in our lives. No matter what the desert looks like, it is there that God has the opportunity to speak to our heart.

*Meditation:* Where is your desert? When was the last time that you spent some time there?

*Prayer:* God of the desert, once you led the Hebrew people to the desert and formed them into your chosen Israelite community. You gave them your Word and your Torah as you spoke to their hearts. Strengthen our feeble hands and make firm our weak knees that we may walk the highway of your holy way. Calm our fears. Open our blind eyes to see your works; clear our deaf ears to hear your Word; loosen our tongues to sing your praise. Come and save us, for we await your glory and splendor to be revealed in the Second Coming of your Son, our Lord Jesus Christ, who lives and reigns with you and the Holy Spirit, one God, for ever and ever. Amen.

# Tuesday
## Prepare the Way

In the desert prepare the way of the LORD!
Make straight in the wasteland a highway for our God!
Every valley shall be filled in,
every mountain and hill shall be made low;
The rugged land shall be made a plain,
the rough country, a broad valley.

(Isaiah 40:3-4)

*Scripture:* Isaiah 40:1-10; Matthew 18:12-14

*Reflection:* When construction begins on a new highway, various types of equipment are hauled to the construction site on flatbed trucks. Caterpillars are unloaded and begin to cut into the earth. Shovels raise buckets of dirt and rock and place these in dump trucks, which haul the earth to another location.

Trees are axed and removed. Slabs of rock are drilled and scaled off. In effect, mountains are leveled and the valleys in between are filled in. The roadbed is prepared with care. Finally, the cement is poured and the pavement is ready to be marked with yellow and white stripes.

For some people, life can seem like a deserted place with no roads to God. They effectively isolate themselves so that there can be no inroads in their lives. Too much work, too much eating, too much drinking, too much smoking, too much depression, and too little sleep: These are the mountains and valleys that need to be leveled and filled in.

The prophet Isaiah shouts, "Here is your God! Here comes with power the Lord God. Prepare his way through your desert!" Like the beginning of work on a new highway, construction in our personal lives means work. The mountains of the Christmas parties and card-writing may need leveling. The valleys of the end-of-the-year blahs may need filling in. Just as we cannot drive a car where there is no highway, so God cannot come to us unless we prepare the road.

*Meditation:* In your life, what mountains need to be leveled? What valleys need to be filled?

*Prayer:* God of the highway, you rule with your strong arm, yet you speak tenderly to us and expiate our guilt. You reveal to all people your glory. Fill in the valleys of depression; level the mountains of pride. Like a shepherd feed us, gather us in your arms, and carry us in your bosom as we prepare for the coming in glory of Jesus, your Son, who is Lord for ever and ever. Amen.

# Wednesday
# Acknowledge Equality

To whom can you liken me as an equal?
    says the Holy One.

(Isaiah 40:25)

*Scripture:* Isaiah 40:25-31; Matthew 11:28-30

*Reflection:* The word "equal" or one of its many synonyms such as "fair," "just," or "right" is used constantly by most people. The Constitution of the United States is based on the presupposition that all people are created equal.

Two children can be observed dividing a candy bar equally. Two adults share a luncheon and divide the bill equally. Two college students often split the chores in their "dorm" room equally. Husbands and wives pledge marriage vows to each other equally. With a little reflection, it is easy to see how often "equal" is used.

Some people often wonder why such a lofty principle as equality does not work. If all are equal, why are there poor people, aliens, orphans, unemployed persons? The fact is that we are not all equal. It is not that the presupposition of equality is wrong, it is the application that is maladjusted.

Every person differs in talents, skills, intelligence, personality, tolerance levels, income, personal needs, and in countless other ways. In fact, about the only time that human beings come close to any sense of equality is during a time of crisis, natural disaster, or death.

All persons are equal in human dignity before God. Some people erroneously believe that there are those who are "more equal" than others, or that they are even equal to God; but this only demonstrates how unequal they really are.

No one is equal to God — not even Satan, who is evil itself. What would the world be like if there were two "superpowers": God and Satan?

God is our Creator; he alone is eternal. Our ability to recognize this is the first step on our way to acknowledge the equality of all and our own place in the great scheme of things.

---

*Meditation:* What experiences can you recall where you experienced authentic equality between people?

*Prayer:* Unequaled God, you are eternal; you are the creator of the whole world. You encourage the fainthearted and you strengthen the weak-kneed. Those who hope in you renew their strength. Help us to soar as on eagles' wings to your understanding of equality. As we prepare for the coming in glory of your Son, Jesus, enable us to run without growing weary and to walk without growing faint. Hear this prayer through Christ our Lord. Amen.

## Thursday
## Shared Power

I am the LORD, your God,
   who grasp your right hand;
It is I who say to you, "Fear not,
   I will help you."
   . . . I will help you, says the LORD;
   your redeemer is the Holy One of Israel.
                                    (Isaiah 41:13-14)

*Scripture:* Isaiah 41:13-20; Matthew 11:11-15

*Reflection:* While a few people may be ambidextrous, most are either dominant on the right or on the left, that is, most people are either right-handed or left-handed. Even those who are ambidextrous have a preference for either the right hand or the left hand when they write, reach out — whatever action they perform.

In the Scriptures the right hand, the right arm, the right side, the right seat, is the place of power. To be grasped by the right hand, as Isaiah states, is to share in the power of God.

What is this power? It is a strength to care for the afflicted and the needy. It is the ability to be a co-creator of life and share life-giving gifts.

A person shares in the power of God by visiting the rivers and fountains of the ill in hospitals, the home-bound, and those in nursing homes. Restored friendships turn deserts to marshes when God's power is shared. Anyone who can share a cup of coffee and make a new friend or just listen to another tell his or her story can plant a tree of God's power that grows for a long time.

It makes no difference whether we are right-handed or left-handed. The power that God shares with us is to be used creatively to give and to sustain life, just as God uses his power creatively to give and to sustain life.

*Meditation:* Today, what can you do with your right/left hand to co-create with God and sustain life?

*Prayer:* Holy One of Israel, our Redeemer, you who stretch out your right hand toward us and share your power with us, do your works in us so that the afflicted and the needy and the thirsty may find rivers and fountains and springs of your grace. Do not forsake us, but turn the desert of our fears into marshlands. May we grow like the cedar in your sight and be as rich as the olive. Help us to know and to understand that you are the one who works wonders in our lives, as we wait for the coming in glory of your Son, Jesus, who sits at your right hand for ever and ever. Amen.

# Friday
# God, Our Teacher

Thus says the LORD, your redeemer,
the Holy One of Israel:
I, the LORD, your God,
teach you what is for your good,
and lead you on the way you should go.
(Isaiah 48:17)

*Scripture:* Isaiah 48:17-19; Matthew 11:16-19

*Reflection:* Teachers shape the world. Scarcely a moment of time is spent without contact with them in some way or another: from the early days of nursery care to preschool, grade school, high school, college, and postgraduate school.

Parents are teachers of correct behavior, moral codes, and manners. Friends teach trust, understanding, and reliability. Specialness, warmth, and wisdom are learned from grandparents. Those who demonstrate vacuum cleaners, cars, and household appliances are teachers. Those labeled as "trainers" are teachers. It is almost impossible to look around the world and not see someone teaching another person something.

God is our teacher, according to the prophet Isaiah. He teaches us through the commandments, God's Word, and other people. He teaches what is good, and he leads us where we need to go.

*Meditation:* Most recently, what has another person taught you? What has God taught you?

*Prayer:* Teaching God, you are our Redeemer; you are the Holy One of Israel. You teach us what is for our good, and you lead us on the way we should go. Make our lives as prosperous as a river, our justice like the waves of the sea. Help us to hear you and to do your will, so that our names are not blotted out from your presence as we await the coming in glory of your Son, Jesus, who is Lord for ever and ever. Amen.

## Saturday
## God's Fire

Like a fire there appeared the prophet
  whose words were as a flaming furnace.
By God's word he shut up the heavens
  and three times brought down fire.
How awesome are you, ELIJAH!
You were taken aloft in a whirlwind,
  in a chariot with fiery horses
                    (Sirach 48:1,3-4,9)

*Scripture:* Sirach 48:1-4,9-11; Matthew 17:10-13

*Reflection:* Like a fire, the Old Testament prophet, Elijah, appeared. A fire draws people to itself; when people see smoke, they rush toward it, for they "know" there must be a fire. A fire warms, heats homes, illuminates the darkness, scares away the shadows and the animals of the night, cooks meals, and creates community from those who gather around it. A fire can also scorch, burn, and sear.

Elijah was like a fire — a prophetic fire. His words burned and his lifestyle seared people. He was a man on fire with God. Elijah demonstrated the flaming power of God.

Because of his fiery personality, Elijah was expected to return before the "day of the Lord," that time when God would rescue his people forever. The gospel writers portray John the Baptizer as Elijah, who returned to prepare the way for the coming day of Jesus. In this way the Old Testament belief concerning Elijah's return was fulfilled in the Baptizer.

We do not have to dress, speak, and act like Elijah and John the Baptizer; but as followers of Christ, we have an obligation to imitate the loving fire of their hearts to the best of our ability.

*Meditation:* Who prepared the way for the coming of the Lord into your life?

*Prayer:* God of fire, you manifested your light in your prophets, Elijah and John the Baptizer. Elijah called upon your name and you sent fire to vindicate your presence. John prepared the way for the coming of your Son, Jesus. Now, gathered by your Spirit around the fire of your love, we watch and hope for the day when Jesus will return in glory. Continue to illumine our darkness and fan into flames a desire to do your will. Bless us with your fiery presence forever. We ask this through Christ our Lord. Amen.

## December 12
### FEAST OF OUR LADY OF GUADALUPE
### Rejoice With Mary

Sing and rejoice, O daughter Zion! See, I am coming to dwell among you, says the LORD.

(Zechariah 2:14)

*Scripture:* Zechariah 2:14-17 or Revelation 11:19; 12:1-6,10; Luke 1:39-47

*Reflection:* Who is "daughter Zion"? A daughter is the female child of parents. Zechariah, however, uses the word "daughter" as a collective name for the people of Israel. Taken together, the Israelites are considered to be God's daughter.

Zion is the mountain upon which the temple in Jerusalem was built. The temple was the center for the Israelites. It represented the dwelling place of God. It was understood that God lived in the temple just as God had lived in a tent when the people wandered the desert.

Through the prophet Zechariah, God speaks. He declares that God's people, God's daughter, should sing and rejoice because God dwells, lives, with people, just as a daughter lives with her parents.

The Virgin Mary is God's special daughter. Mary was chosen from among all women on the earth to be God's dwelling place. In her womb, God came to live in the Incarnation of Jesus, the only Son of God. Mary became a temple, a dwelling place for God in the Spirit and in the flesh.

In the Old Testament, God's presence in the temple was signified by clouds and smoke. In the New Testament, God's presence is seen in the flesh of God's Son. In the present, we recall his presence in the person of his Mother under her various titles. Today we rejoice with Mary under her title of Our Lady of Guadalupe.

*Meditation:* In what way has God made you his daughter?

*Prayer:* Our Father, once you chose a people and you blessed them with your presence in their temple on Mount Zion. From all women on the earth you chose Mary, your daughter, to be the mother of your only Son, Jesus Christ. In Jesus you became present to us in human flesh. Enable us to sing and rejoice for such a great deed as we await the Second Coming in glory of your Christ, who is Lord for ever and ever. Amen.

# Third Sunday of Advent

# Cycle A
## Fear Not!

Be strong, fear not!
Here is your God,
  he comes with vindication;
With divine recompense
  he comes to save you.
                    (Isaiah 35:4)

*Scripture:* Isaiah 35:1-6,10; James 5:7-10; Matthew 11:2-11

*Reflection:* Fear is a terrible feeling. It keeps people from respond-
ing, causing them to freeze and revert to a primitive stance of
defense. Fear debilitates and incapacitates. People cannot respond
as they would want to if they are afraid.

Fears abound. Some persons worry about making airline con-
nections and, then, about a safe flight. Others fear illness for
themselves and family members. Parents fear drugs and alcohol
abuse and worry about the sexual activity of their children. Fear
causes trembling hands and weak knees. It keeps people away
from others; it isolates.

Isaiah proclaims that God comes and eliminates fear. God
fosters trust; where there is trust, there is no fear. Trust of God
fosters faith in God. Trust of others fosters faith in others. Fear
fosters trust in self alone.

In a moment of fear we may feel that if we want something done
right, we must do it ourselves — we can't trust or count on anyone

else. Those of us who think this way should take Isaiah's words to heart: "Be strong, fear not!"

*Meditation:* What fear is currently isolating you? In what ways can you trust that God will show you the way?

*Prayer:* Faithful God, you strengthen the hands that tremble, and you make firm the knees that are weak. To those who are frightened you say, "Be strong!" and "Fear not!" Teach us to trust, to believe, in you. We ask you to come with vindication, with your divine recompense, and save us in the second advent of Jesus, your Son, in glory, for he is Lord for ever and ever. Amen.

## Cycle B
## Robed in Justice

I rejoice heartily in the LORD,
    in my God is the joy of my soul;
For he has clothed me with a robe of salvation,
    and wrapped me in a mantle of justice,
Like a bridegroom adorned with a diadem,
    like a bride bedecked with her jewels.
                                    (Isaiah 61:10)

*Scripture:* Isaiah 61:1-2,10-11; 1 Thessalonians 5:16-24; John 1:6-8,19-28

*Reflection:* To be clothed or wrapped is to be enfolded. A mother carefully wraps her newborn child in a blanket and tucks in the corners. A gift-giver wraps a package while smoothing the corners, applying tape, and tying the ribbon and bow in just the right place. Adults clothe themselves in bathrobes both before and after showers, to relax and to feel snugly warm. Robed in parental love, children make their way in the world. People, enfolded in friendship, are able to face tough situations and emerge as winners.

God reaches out and wraps the world in salvation and justice. Through salvation, he rescues people when they are ready to be rescued. Through justice, he teaches them how to live and care for each other. God does not force his robe on his children; he stands like a valet, holding the robe of salvation and justice, ever ready to slip it on those who are ready.

This realization should make each one of us rejoice heartily in the Lord, who is the joy of our souls.

*Meditation:* What is your most recent experience of God enfolding, clothing, or wrapping you in salvation and justice?

*Prayer:* Gift-giving God, you clothe us with the robe of salvation, you wrap us in the mantle of justice, and you anoint us with your Spirit. Send us out with gifts of glad tidings to the lowly, healing for the brokenhearted, liberty for captives, release for prisoners, and the announcement of your year of favor for all. May we wait in joyful hope for the coming in glory of the bridegroom, your Son, Jesus the anointed One, who is Lord for ever and ever. Amen.

## Cycle C
## Exult in the Lord

Shout for joy, O daughter Zion!
  sing joyfully, O Israel!
Be glad and exult with all your heart,
  O daughter Jerusalem!
The LORD has removed the judgment against you,
  he has turned away your enemies;
The King of Israel, the LORD, is in your midst,
  you have no further misfortune to fear.

(Zephaniah 3:14-15)

*Scripture:* Zephaniah 3:14-18; Philippians 4:4-7; Luke 3:10-18

*Reflection:* Happy persons are filled with peace; they overflow with joy. Likewise, those who stand in the presence of the ones they love take on an aura of happiness and enthusiasm. They cannot hold the joy in or pretend that it is not there; it is clearly visible to all — much as stripes and plaids visually clash when worn together.

The same phenomenon exists when people are filled with the presence of the Lord. At peace with God, they exude the aroma of the Lord. Their whole attitude toward living is affected.

Zephaniah attempts to capture this joy in words by shouting and singing gleefully, being glad, and exulting with the heart. Why? Because when we are truly absorbed by the presence of the Lord, we overflow with joy.

*Meditation:* What was your most recent experience of the Lord's presence that caused you to overflow, shout, sing, and exult with joy?

*Prayer:* King of Israel, mighty Savior, God who is ever-present with your people, you make us shout for joy and sing joyfully in your sight. You make us glad and cause us to exult with all our hearts. Enable us to shout the good news of your love, to sing of your forgiveness and mercy, and to exult with all our hearts at the coming in glory of your Son, Jesus Christ, who is Lord for ever and ever. Amen.

## Monday
## Follow the Star

I see him, though not now;
    I behold him, though not near:
A star shall advance from Jacob,
    and a staff shall rise from Israel. . . .
                    (Numbers 24:17)

*Scripture:* Jeremiah 23:5-8; Matthew 1:18-24

*Reflection:* Stars shine all day and all night. However, the brightness of the sun prevents their being seen in the day, and they can only be glimpsed during a clear night. People look up to stars — both those in the sky and those persons who are called stars —

because they shine so outstandingly in their field of expertise. There are movie stars, television stars, as well as stellar writers, novelists, journalists, and leaders. Starlight streams from singers, bands, and orchestras. In Hollywood, prominent actors are known by the star on their doors and their name in neon lights.

The author of the Book of Numbers, in quoting Balaam's prophecy about a star advancing from Jacob, saw the rising of an outstanding person from the tribe of Jacob who would be a great leader. His light would not radiate from the sky but from his ability to lead the people. And not only one star-studded leader emerged, but a host of them. Later generations viewed Joseph, David, and Solomon as stars that had risen at the right time in history to lead the people.

Today we too admire these stars of the past, but we follow with all our hearts the Star of stars, Jesus Christ himself.

*Meditation:* Who is a star for you?

*Prayer:* God of the stars, you reveal yourself in every generation through the light of countless men and women. You guided your people, Israel, watching over their tents, making them like gardens planted near streams of flowing water. You gave them kingly leaders, whose royalty even you exalted. Enlighten our darkness. Open our eyes to see the truth. Send us your greatest star, Jesus, whom we see, though not now, whom we behold, though not near, for we wait for him to come in glory as the Morning Star. He is Lord for ever and ever. Amen.

# Tuesday
# Faithful Remnant

I will leave as a remnant in your midst
  a people humble and lowly,
Who shall take refuge in the name of the LORD:
  the remnant of Israel.

(Zephaniah 3:12)

*Scripture:* Judges 13:2-7,24-25; Luke 1:5-25

*Reflection:* In clothing stores there is usually a table with pieces of cloth of various lengths and colors. This table is called a remnant table, and the pieces of cloth are called remnants. The small piece of cloth that is left on a bolt after most of the cloth has been sold is called a remnant.

There are remnants in groups of people, too. The last two or three in an old social group are remnants of past gatherings. The last two or three who refuse to go with the majority of the crowd are remnants of how things used to be. Christian martyrs were remnants of faithful people.

Zephaniah proclaimed that God would leave a remnant of the people of Israel. A few would take refuge in God; these would do no wrong, speak no lies, and practice no deceit. This remnant would not be just what was left over; it would be the best part of all — those faithful to their God. We too must remain faithful to God, as humble remnants of God's chosen ones.

*Meditation:* How are you a faithful remnant?

*Prayer:* God of the remnant, you take delight in your faithful people. Purify our lips that we may call upon your name and find refuge in you, as we wait for the coming in glory of Jesus, your Son, who lives and reigns with you and the Holy Spirit, one God, for ever and ever. Amen.

## Wednesday
## God's Justice

Let justice descend, O heavens, like dew from above,
    like gentle rain let the skies drop it down.
Let the earth open and salvation bud forth;
    let justice also spring up!

(Isaiah 45:8)

*Scripture:* Isaiah 7:10-14; Luke 1:26-38

*Reflection:* Most people, when they hear the word *justice,* think of synonyms such as *fair* or *right.* To them, justice means not being cheated. It is pictured as the blindfolded lady holding the balanced scales or the court room with the judge behind the high bench who renders justice by deciding aright. These are examples of legal justice.

According to the prophet Isaiah, biblical justice comes from God; it is like dew which forms on the morning grass; it is like gentle rain which the skies drop down; it is like a seed which springs up from the earth, grows, and blossoms.

God creates justice, and his justice is salvation. He rescues people; he delivers them from famine and oppression. God's justice consists of care for the widow, the alien, and the orphan, and he expects the same concern for others from those who claim to be his people.

We know there is no other God than the God of justice. And it behooves us to practice his kind of authentic justice.

*Meditation:* In what way have you most recently manifested God's type of justice?

*Prayer:* God of justice, you are the Lord; there is no other. You form the light, and you create the darkness. You design the heavens and the earth as a dwelling place for your people. There is no just and saving God but you. Turn us toward you that we may be safe. Bend our wills to do your will. Loosen our tongues to speak your justice that, like a gentle rain, it may fall from our lips and spring up and blossom throughout the earth. We ask this through Jesus Christ, your Son of justice, whose coming in glory we await. He is Lord for ever and ever. Amen.

# Thursday
## Return to God

The LORD calls you back,
   like a wife forsaken and grieved in spirit,
A wife married in youth and then cast off,
   says your God.
For a brief moment I abandoned you,
   but with great tenderness I will take you back.
In an outburst of wrath, for a moment
   I hid my face from you;
But with enduring love I take pity on you,
   says the LORD, your redeemer.

(Isaiah 54:6-8)

*Scripture:* Songs 2:8-14 or Zephaniah 3:14-18; Luke 1:39-45

*Reflection:* Marriage is used to describe the relationship of God to the Israelites. The people of Israel corporately entered into a marriage covenant with God, the One who is husband and Creator. The vows of the marriage, or the terms of the covenant, consisted of the Decalogue, the Ten Commandments.

Isaiah portrays God as doing battle with God's spouse. God has abandoned her (the Israelites). He is extremely disappointed with the relationship.

Isaiah is stating that Israel had been unfaithful, and this was the cause for God's abandonment. God, however, remains faithful. All that was needed was for God's spouse to repent, to turn around, to convert, and to demonstrate that she would be faithful once again. In the moment of conversion, God would take her back and remove her shame.

Today, through Baptism we enter into a marriage covenant with God. The marriage vows consist of the baptismal promises made on the day of Baptism, renewed yearly during the Easter Vigil and on Easter Sunday, and stated weekly in the Profession of Faith. If we break our vows, we must convert and demonstrate that we will be faithful once again. God is always ready and willing to remove our shame and receive us as his bride.

*Meditation:* How have you been faithful to your baptismal vows? How have you been unfaithful to them?

*Prayer:* God of faithfulness, when we sin, you call us back, like a wife forsaken and grieved in spirit. For only a brief moment you abandon us, so that with great tenderness you can take us back. Do not hide your face. With your enduring love pity us. Holy One of Israel, our husband and our Creator, our Redeemer, keep us faithful as we await the coming in glory of your Son, Jesus Christ, who is Lord for ever and ever. Amen.

# Friday
## Healing Divisions

The foreigners who join themselves to the LORD,
  ministering to him,
Loving the name of the LORD,
  and becoming his servants . . .
Them I will bring to my holy mountain
  and make joyful in my house of prayer . . .
For my house shall be called
  a house of prayer for all peoples.
Thus says the LORD GOD,
  who gathers the dispersed of Israel:
Others will I gather to him
  besides those already gathered.

(Isaiah 56:6-8)

*Scripture:* 1 Samuel 1:24-28; Luke 1:46-46

*Reflection:* In every country there are many who are called foreigners, aliens, boat people, refugees, immigrants. All of these names serve to separate and divide people into two groups — them and us.

In the time of the prophet Isaiah, the foreigner was anyone who was not an Israelite, one of Hebrew origin.

Other types of "foreigners" exist today besides those listed above. Segregation based on the color of skin, sexual preferences, business dealings, the home, income, intelligence, education — to name a few — create new types of foreigners.

The prophet Isaiah proclaims that foreigners who keep the covenant, into which they were not even initiated, will be brought to God's holy mountains, Horeb and Zion, the places where God lived. Those who are called "them" will worship with "us" in the temple, the Lord's house of prayer.

We cannot make separations or distinctions in the eyes of God. All people are equal in human dignity. God's house is a house of prayer for all of us. No one is excluded from his house, as he keeps gathering others into the fold. God seeks unity and not division among us all.

*Meditation:* Who is labeled as a "foreigner" in your everyday life?

*Prayer:* God of foreigners, you gather all people to yourself that they might minister to you, love your name, become your servants, and keep your covenant. Heal the divisions that separate us one from another. Bring us to your holy mountain and make us joyful in your house of prayer. Make us ready for your salvation which is about to come and for your justice which is about to be revealed in Jesus Christ, whose glorious coming we await. He is Lord for ever and ever. Amen.

## December 17
## Signs of Power

Judah, like a lion's whelp,
> you have grown up on prey, my son.
He crouches like a lion recumbent,
> the king of beasts — who would dare rouse him?
The scepter shall never depart from Judah,
> or the mace from between his legs. . . .

(Genesis 49:9-10)

*Scripture:* Genesis 49:2,8-10; Matthew 1:1-17

*Reflection:* The author of Genesis presents three signs of power —
the lion, the scepter, and the mace. The lion has always been
considered as the king of the beasts, the king of the jungle, because
he is dominant and instills fear in all other creatures. The lion is
ever ready to spring upon his prey and to devour it.

The scepter is a staff or a baton that is borne by a sovereign as an
emblem of authority. Most often kings and queens carry such
instruments when exercising some royal function.

A mace is a heavy, often spiked, staff or club that is used for
breaking armor. It is a weapon that is used in war.

These three power signs are used by the author of Genesis to
insure and to justify the dominant position of the tribe of Judah
among the other eleven tribes of Israel throughout history. The
author makes it clear that the line of Judean kings, rulers, and
leaders will continue.

Contemporary signs of power have changed little from the day that the Genesis author wrote the words recorded here. Police carry sticks and guns. Chairpersons and presidents of companies wield their gavels at meetings. In many ecclesiastical circles, bishops carry pastoral staffs. Keys are treated with great respect because they open doors, safety deposit boxes, file cabinets, and offices. Nuclear warheads perched on top of missiles can pierce the armor of the entire planet.

The signs of power mentioned here have not always been used properly in the past. Our task today is to accept them gingerly and use them wisely.

*Meditation:* What are some of the signs of your power and authority?

*Prayer:* God of power and might, you govern your people with justice and bring forth peace from the mountains. Make justice flower in our day and make peace the object of all our power plays in the present. May we always acknowledge your rule from sea to sea and to the ends of the earth. May the name of your Son, Jesus, be blessed forever; and may his name remain ever on our lips as we wait for his coming in glory. He is Lord for ever and ever. Amen.

## December 18
## Promises Kept

Behold, the days are coming, says the LORD,
    when I will raise up a righteous shoot to David;
As king he shall reign and govern wisely,
    he shall do what is just and right in the land.
                                    (Jeremiah 23:5)

*Scripture:* Jeremiah 23:5-8; Matthew 1:18-24

*Reflection:* A day hardly goes by without one person making some kind of promise to another one. "I will pick that up at the store." "Yes, I will mail your letter." "Can I stop at the bank on my way home? Of course, I can!" "I promise that I will not tell him." "I assure you that I will go and see her." "I will do the favor I promised in just a moment."

Because of the plurality of the promises that are made in a day, one may find it difficult to keep all of them. Most promises are made without a consideration given to the limitations of time, human energy, ability, and possibility.

God made a two-part promise, as Jeremiah records here. He promised first of all to provide a king in David's line. This monarch would be more than just a reigning sovereign; he would be the incarnation of justice. God also promised a second exodus. The first had been the escape from Egypt. The second would be the escape from Babylon, the "land of the north." Just as the first bestowed freedom on the people, so the second would set them free on their own land.

God kept the promises he made. He raised up Davidic heirs who led the people, and he saw to it that the Israelites returned from Babylonian exile to rebuild the temple in Jerusalem. We too must keep the promises we have made at our Baptism and Confirmation.

*Meditation:* What promise(s) have you most recently made and kept?

*Prayer:* God of promises, once through your servant Moses you led your people from slavery in the land of Egypt to freedom in a land flowing with milk and honey. In later days, when your people were banished from their land, you raised up Cyrus, King of Persia, who set your people free. Continue to keep your promises. Today, raise up righteous shoots of justice that we may be saved and dwell in your security as we watch and wait for the coming in glory of your Son, Jesus Christ, who is Lord for ever and ever. Amen.

# Fourth Sunday of Advent

## Cycle A
## Signs of God's Presence

Ask for a sign from the LORD, your God; let it be deep as the nether world, or high as the sky!

(Isaiah 7:11)

*Scripture:* Isaiah 7:10-14; Romans 1:1-7; Matthew 1:18-24

*Reflection:* Depths and heights fascinate most people. Some individuals are enthralled by the depths of the ocean: The undersea world contains creatures never seen before. Crystal-clear waters make visible the small animals of the sea. Other persons prefer to explore the caves of the earth. A spelunker will walk, crawl, or scoot into a dark womb of the earth. Ancient gorges carved by the constant flow of rivers call others to explore them. The Grand Canyon, the Black Canyon, and the Royal Gorge leave people breathless as they view the stringlike rivers from their rims.

The heights are attained by those who are willing to face the elements of wind, rain, sleet, and snow in order to climb a mountain. Every climber wants to reach the summit of the highest mountain someday. If the heights cannot be reached on foot, then airplanes, spacecraft, and rockets beckon other adventurers. In the past, trips to the moon satisfied this desire; now, a shuttle service throughout the universe is contemplated.

This human fascination with both depths and heights can offer people signs of God's presence. These experiences, obviously, are not common for most persons; they are the exceptions. However, they do remind all people that sometimes God's revelation can be missed in the simple or the strange.

God called Abraham to leave his country and go to a new land. The sign given to Abraham was circumcision — a rather strange indication of God's presence. God called Moses to lead the Hebrew people from Egyptian slavery to a promised land of freedom, a land flowing with milk and honey. The sign given to Moses was a burning bush — again, a rather strange indication of God's presence.

Throughout time God has called people to look forward to the future with hope. The sign given was a virgin with child — an even stranger indication of God's presence. What we should note for our own further instruction is that the name of this child was to be Immanuel, which means God-with-us; the child was to be the presence of God — not just a sign of God's presence. This thought should raise our spirits from the depths to the heights if we ever are tempted to doubt God's presence in our midst.

*Meditation:* What recent depth, height, or ordinary experience did God use to reveal his presence to you?

*Prayer:* God of the universe, you are present in the depths and the heights in uncounted ways. The signs of your love abound. Your greatest sign of love was the personal presence of Jesus, your Son, who is Immanuel, the incarnation of your Godhead. Help us to recognize the signs that you give us of his coming in glory, for Jesus is Lord for ever and ever. Amen.

## Cycle B
## Temples of God

[David] said to Nathan the prophet, ''Here I am living in a house of cedar, while the ark of God dwells in a tent!'' Nathan answered the king . . . ''The Lord . . . reveals to you that he will establish a house for you. Your house and your kingdom shall endure forever before me; your throne shall stand firm forever.''

(2 Samuel 7:2-3,11,16)

*Scripture:* 2 Samuel 7:1-5,8-11,16; Romans 16:25-27; Luke 1:26-38

*Reflection:* House construction is a common enough sight. Almost every person has driven through a neighborhood and observed new homes being built. Wood, stone, and metal are combined to provide a structure for human habitation.

David, the greatest King of Israel, once he had defeated his enemies and pushed back the borders of his kingdom on all sides, built a palace, a house, for himself. After he had settled into his house of cedar, he realized that the ark, the sign of God's presence with the people, was in a tent. So he decided that God, who had made David great, should have a house to live in. David began to collect the materials that would be required to build a temple for God.

God, however, as so often happens, had other plans. He did not need a house. In fact, he would establish a house for David. His kingdom would endure forever, and his throne would be firm.

David would not do the house-building; God would construct the temple out of David's flesh and blood.

God does not live in houses made of wood, stone, or metal. He lives in the houses God creates. He dwells in us. Each one of us is a dwelling place, a house, a temple, for God.

*Meditation:* What is your most recent experience of God living in your house?

*Prayer:* God of builders, you established the house of David, your chosen king, that his kingdom might endure forever before you and that his throne might stand firm forever in your sight. We are your creatures, temples meant for your dwelling. Come and live in us and keep us watchful for the day of the Second Coming in glory of your Son, Jesus, who was born of the line of David and who is Lord for ever and ever. Amen.

# Cycle C
# Place of Origin

But you, Bethlehem-Ephrathah,
    too small to be among the clans of Judah,
From you shall come forth for me
    one who is to be ruler in Israel;
Whose origin is from of old,
    from ancient times.

(Micah 5:1)

*Scripture:* Micah 5:1-4; Hebrews 10:5-10; Luke 1:39-45

*Reflection:* What can be smaller than a small town? Some people would say that a village in the country is smaller than a small town. More often than not, any place where people choose to live somewhat near each other but certainly not in a "city situation" is referred to as "the sticks" or "the woods." Humorously, people state that the entering and leaving signs for such places can be nailed to the same pole. Others conclude that if people blink as they drive through such a place, they will undoubtedly miss it. Smaller-than-small towns are designated as dots on a map or not even a dot on a map. In comparison to a city, a smaller-than-small town is "nowheresville."

Bethlehem was such a place, if the word "place" can be used to describe it! The prophet Micah had to use its old name, Ephrathah, so that his readers would know the area to which he was referring. Bethlehem-Ephrathah was no place, no city; it was "no-wheresville" and of no importance whatsoever. All of this means that it was a perfect place for the God who appears in the strangest of places and does wonders beyond imagining and calls the strangest people to participate in what at first look like ridiculous plans.

Out of Bethlehem-Ephrathah there came the shepherd son of Jesse, who later became known in history as King David. In order to make the Davidic connection, both Matthew and Luke locate the birth of Jesus in Bethlehem. This helps to seal the Davidic line problem (if Jesus' father is God and his foster father is Joseph, then how can he be of David's line?) for the Messiah, who was supposed to be a descendant from David's family tree.

Today, God continues to appear in the strangest of places; he constantly does wonders for us — by asking us to participate in what at first seem to be crazy plans. Any place that is considered to be "nowheresville" is a prime spot for God's revelation to take place. He seems to lure us to places that aren't even dots on the map.

*Meditation:* What was the most recent occasion of God's appearance to you in a strange place, in some strange wonder, or in some request to be a part of a strange plan?

*Prayer:* Unpredictable God, from Bethlehem-Ephrathah you brought forth the shepherd, David, to rule your people, Israel. He stood firm and was leader of the flock by your strength and in the majesty of your name. From Bethlehem-Ephrathah you raised up the eternal shepherd, your Son, Jesus, who leads us on our journey. Give us patience to wait and give us eyes to look in strange places for the coming in glory of him whose origin is from of old, from ancient times, for he is Lord for ever and ever. Amen.

## December 19
## Roots

An angel of the LORD appeared to the woman [the wife of Manoah] and said to her, "Though you are barren and have had no children, yet you will conceive and bear a son."

(Judges 13:3)

*Scripture:* Judges 13:2-7,24-25; Luke 1:5-25

*Reflection:* A woman who is barren is one who is incapable of conceiving a child; however, this is a limited meaning of the word. In primitive biological understanding, man implanted his seed in woman, who functioned as a ten-month incubator. The woman had no part in contributing to the newly conceived life; the man had planted the child, as one would plant a seed, where it would grow and mature. Primitive people did not understand biology as it is understood today.

In an expanded sense, barren can refer to the inability to bring forth life of any kind. Physical sterility does not imply barrenness in this expanded meaning of the word. Many people are able to give birth to life from within themselves and share it with others, while others find themselves without this gift — barren. Barrenness can be healed with a smile that evokes life from another, with a few kind words such as ''Thank you,'' with a short note or letter, with a favor. Individuals who find themselves in a barren time may use a few moments of prayer, relaxation, time with another, or time with God to conceive new life.

If we remain barren, we are without life. We never have time for our own needs; we are always living for the next day instead of living today. We have no time for others; we do not give and share. However, if we are willing to stand before God and admit our barrenness, we often discover that our barren condition is turned into fruitful life.

*Meditation:* In what way(s) are you barren — without life? In what way(s) are you fruitful — overflowing with life?

*Prayer:* God of the barren, you turn emptiness into fullness, sadness into joy, and childlessness into sons and daughters. Touch our empty wombs. Implant in us the seeds of your grace that we might give birth to the eternal life you promise, as we wait for the glorious coming of your Son, Jesus the Christ, who is Lord for ever and ever. Amen.

## December 20
## Signs From God

The LORD spoke to Ahaz: Ask for a sign from the LORD, your God; let it be deep as the nether world, or high as the sky! . . . The Lord himself will give you this sign: the virgin shall be with child, and bear a son, and shall name him Immanuel.

(Isaiah 7:10-11,14)

*Scripture:* Isaiah 7:10-14; Luke 1:26-38

*Reflection:* Signs are familiar to all people. Everywhere there are signs that have been erected, pasted, posted, grounded, and lighted. Road signs give directions, distances, and cautions. Hotel signs invite weary travelers to break for the night. Food signs suggest to people where they should consider eating.

Like primitive peoples, modern persons look for religious signs. Today people want signs from God. They want them because they believe that these signs will tell them what they ought to do. Sometimes people want them in order to confirm as right the answer which they have reached.

It is surprising how many signs God actually gives. However, people do not recognize them because they are often strange and do not fall into the usual realm of vision or expectation.

Isaiah records the sign given to King Ahaz: The virgin shall be with child and bear a son. This is certainly not a common sign; a woman giving birth to a son is not a virgin. Who would recognize this as a sign from God? Most people would doubt that such an event could happen. The first cry from people would be that the so-called virgin is not a virgin anymore. And, of course, this would indicate that those who make such a statement have missed the sign.

Throughout our lives God gives signs, if we have the eyes to see them, the ears to hear them, and the common sense to recognize them. All of the signs that God gives can be contained in the one word — Immanuel. Why? Because "Immanuel" means "God-with-us." Who could possibly want any other sign?

*Meditation:* Has God given you any recent signs to indicate that he is with you?

*Prayer:* God of signs, to you belong the earth and its fullness; the whole world and all people are yours. You surround our days with signs of your love. Open our eyes to see you in all of creation. Open our ears to hear you in the whispers of the night. May we touch you in the life we share with others. Give us joy as we seek your face and prepare for the coming in glory of the incarnate sign of your presence, Immanuel, your Son, Jesus Christ, who lives and reigns with you and the Holy Spirit, one God, for ever and ever. Amen.

# December 21
# God of Love
# (First Option)

Hark! my lover — here he comes
  springing across the mountains,
leaping across the hills.
My lover speaks; he says to me,
  "Arise, my beloved, my beautiful one,
  and come!"

(Song of Songs 2:8,10)

*Scripture:* Songs 2:8-14; Luke 1:39-45

*Reflection:* When people "fall" in love, they, even if it is stated in the least radical of ways, are crazily, wildly in love. All the lover wants is time and more time to be with the one who is loved. Lovers make time for lunch, for evening movies, for play, for music, for just being present to each other. Both lovers are caught up in each other; they drown in each other's love. Some refer to this as "madness."

The author of the Song of Songs captures this all-consuming love in his poem about two people in love. This type of love can be compared to God's love for people; he is in love with people. He is like a young colt, who playfully runs up and down the mountains and hills in an effort to get his lover's attention.

God's love for us is wild and crazy and, from a human point of view, ridiculous. A human lover who gets no response might give up, but God never quits. He pursues us relentlessly, even more so than human lovers do. God is madly in love with us.

*Meditation:* What is your most recent experience of God's overwhelming love for you?

*Prayer:* God of love, you spring across the mountains, you leap across the hills, you stand behind our walls, you gaze through our windows — so much do you love us. Come and take us by the hand. Let us see you in the faces of those we love. Let us hear your voice in the voices of those we love. Make us ready for the coming in glory of your Son whom you love, Jesus Christ, who is Lord for ever and ever. Amen.

# December 21
# God's Presence
# (Second Option)

The King of Israel, the LORD, is in your midst,
    you have no further misfortune to fear.
On that day, it shall be said to Jerusalem:
    Fear not, O Zion, be not discouraged!
The LORD, your God, is in your midst,
    a mighty savior;
He will rejoice over you with gladness,
    and renew you in his love,
He will sing joyfully because of you.
(Zephaniah 3:15-17)

*Scripture:* Zephaniah 3:14-18; Luke 1:39-45

*Reflection:* There are many different ways to be present to another. Physically, people can touch each other by holding hands, imparting a kiss, or being in the sight of the other.

Mentally, people can be present to each other by looking at a picture, by remembering a past conversation, or by just thinking of the other. Spiritually, the presence of another can be sensed through prayer or by some extrasensory means.

There is a rare moment when a combination of all types of presence seem to converge. This happens when a child, for example, rests secure in a crib, surrounded by peace, wrapped in faithful trust, basking in rays of love. When does this occur?

This moment happens when people realize that the King of Israel, the Lord, is in their midst. Fear flees like a fox being pursued by hounds in a hunt. Discouragement blows away like dust in a windstorm. Furthermore, God gets so excited about being with people that he rejoices over them.

God is happy to be present to us. He wants to be in our midst and to renew his covenant of love with us. God gets so excited about presence that he wants to sing about it.

*Meditation:* When was your last experience of being filled with peace because you realized that the Lord was in your presence?

*Prayer:* King of Israel, you withhold your judgment against your people, rejoicing over them with gladness, renewing them in your love, and singing joyfully because of them. Remove the fear that keeps us from recognizing your presence in our midst. Send your mighty Savior, Jesus, the Christ, in glory. We ask this through our

Lord, Jesus Christ, your Son, who lives and reigns with you and the Holy Spirit, one God, for ever and ever. Amen.

## December 22
## Dedication

Once he [Samuel] was weaned, she [Hannah] brought him up with her, along with a three-year-old bull, an ephah of flour, and a skin of wine, and presented him at the temple of the LORD in Shiloh. . . . Hannah . . . said: " . . . As long as he lives, he shall be dedicated to the LORD."

(1 Samuel 1:24-25,28)

*Scripture:* 1 Samuel 1:24-28; Luke 1:46-56

*Reflection:* Hannah brought a set of strange gifts to God for the dedication of Samuel! Who would bring a three-year-old bull, an ephah of flour, and a skin of wine in order to present a child to God? Today many people have enough trouble merely bringing a child to the waters of Baptism!

Yet, if examined closely, it can be seen that Hannah's gifts are not so strange after all. The three-year-old bull echoes the covenant-making ceremony between God and Abraham. Abraham split into two pieces " . . . a three-year-old heifer, a three-year-old she-goat, [and] a three-year-old ram" (Genesis 15:9). Through this ritual God and Abraham entered into a covenant. Abraham experienced God. After sunset, when the smoking brazier and flaming torch — signs of God's presence — passed between the pieces of the animals, Abraham experienced an epiphany, a theophany, a manifestation of God.

Hannah's gift of the ephah of flour echoes another Abrahamic experience. When three visitors approach Abraham's tent in the heat of the day, he offers them hospitality, rest, and food. Abraham tells Sarah, "Quick, three seahs of fine flour! Knead it and make rolls" (Genesis 18:6). Three seahs of flour equals one ephah! Abraham discovers that the three visitors are a manifestation of God with a message that he and Sarah will conceive a son.

The ephah of flour is also echoed in the account of Gideon's sacrifice of "a kid and an ephah of flour in the form of unleavened cakes" (Judges 6:19). After preparing and presenting the sacrifice, "the angel of the LORD stretched out the tip of the staff he held, and touched the meat and unleavened cakes. Thereupon a fire came up from the rock which consumed the meat and unleavened cakes" (Judges 6:21). Gideon then realized that he had experienced a theophany, a manifestation of God.

Hannah used the signs of past theophanies in order to dedicate Samuel, who was to be the vehicle for many future epiphanies of God. Samuel would anoint as King of Israel a shepherd boy named David, who would himself begin a line of kings for Israel. The story of Hannah's dedication of Samuel is like a lightning flash of insight: God has dedicated the child to himself.

Today God appears often enough to us. Theophanies continue on mountaintops, in campsites, on the ocean, on the beach, in people who are loved in special ways, in the birth of a child, in Baptism, and in various other ways. At the very moment we dedicate ourselves to doing the will of God, a theophany is taking place: God is present.

*Meditation:* When did you most recently experience a theophany? What was the sign?

*Prayer:* God of Hannah, Samuel, Abraham, Sarah, and Gideon, you have chosen animals and flour and wine to be vehicles of your revelation of yourself to your people. Through the waters of Baptism you have revealed yourself to us and dedicated us to yourself. Help us to know your will and to do it in our lives. Hear our prayer as we wait for the revelation of the glory of the Second Coming of Jesus, your Son, who is Lord for ever and ever. Amen.

## December 23
## God's Messenger

I am sending my messenger
   to prepare the way before me;
And suddenly there will come to the temple
   the LORD whom you seek,
And the messenger of the covenant whom you desire.
Yes, he is coming, says the LORD of hosts.

(Malachi 3:1)

*Scripture:* Malachi 3:1-4,23-24; Luke 1:57-66

*Reflection:* Before the days of the postal service, UPS, telephones, and computers, messages were delivered by people who had to memorize the message. Today this is no longer the case;

telegraphs, satellite dishes, microwave relay, television, and radio have replaced professional message-bearers.

God is constantly sending messages to people. They come in the form of written words such as Scripture, sacred writings, and other books of spiritual reading.

God delivers messages in the person of other people. Like the prophets of old, there are those today who speak the truth of which not even they themselves are aware. Furthermore, many times they never see the results.

God also delivers messages through the world of nature. The fire that refines silver or gold, the sun rising and coursing across the sky, the moon filling the darkness with shadows, the ocean waves dying on the shore — all these events deliver messages from God.

The message that God sends is himself. In a variety of ways, he comes to each and every personal temple; and people find the One they never knew they were seeking by means of the message that God delivers.

When God comes to us, his presence is at once difficult to endure because it is terrible and great, and at the same time it is peacefully pleasing because we can be absorbed in the good news of the message. To stand before God is difficult to endure because there is no way to hide; we can only stand as our authentic selves. Yet, to stand before God is pleasing because we have no mask; we must be present to ourselves in the light of God's truth.

*Meditation:* In what way has God most recently delivered a message to you? What was the message?

*Prayer:* God of the covenant, in times past you sent us messages through your prophets, who spoke and wrote your word for generations yet to be born. Come to us now with your word of truth. Prepare the way in us for the Second Coming in glory of your Son, Jesus, the messenger of your covenant, whom we desire. Help us to endure the great and terrible day of his coming and to stand secure when he appears. He is Lord for ever and ever. Amen.

## December 24
## Greatness Comes From God
## (Morning)

The LORD of hosts has this to say: It was I who took you from the pasture and from the care of the flock to be commander of my people Israel. I have been with you wherever you went, and I have destroyed all your enemies before you. And I will make you famous like the great ones of the earth.

(2 Samuel 7:8-9)

*Scripture:* 2 Samuel 7:1-5,8-11,16; Luke 1:67-79

*Reflection:* Greatness refers to recognition or place or prestige in relationship to other people. It is bestowed on people because they are recognized as having done something which is declared to be of importance. Some people spend their entire lifetimes striving for greatness, and they will do almost anything to get the position or the name that will declare their greatness.

It is easy to forget that authentic greatness comes from God. Such is the message that the prophet Nathan delivered to King

David. It was God, Nathan declares, who took David from the pasture as a shepherd boy and made him into the greatest king of Israel. It was God who went with David and enabled him to destroy his enemies. And it was God who made David famous.

Authentic greatness in the eyes of others is all God's doing. This is an important truth which should not be forgotten. However, what is seen as great in God's eyes may not ever be recognized by others. This, too, must be remembered.

We all possess some degree of greatness because of personal gifts that God has bestowed on us. It matters not how important or nonimportant these are to others; what matters is how important they are to God, the giver of all greatness. This lesson that David had to keep learning throughout his lifetime we must never forget.

*Meditation:* How has God made you great? How has God given you the gift of greatness?

*Prayer:* God of greatness, you took David from the pasture and the care of the flock and made him king of your people, Israel. You traveled with him, destroyed his enemies, and made him famous like the great ones of the earth. In the multiple gifts you have bestowed upon us, may we perceive your greatness all around us. Continue to fill us with your love, as we wait for the coming in glory of your Son, Jesus the Christ, whose kingdom endures, whose throne stands firm for ever and ever. Amen.

# December 24
## Espoused of God
## (Vigil of Christmas)

No more shall men call you "Forsaken,"
  or your land "Desolate,"
But you shall be called "My Delight,"
  and your land "Espoused."
                              (Isaiah 62:4)

*Scripture:* Isaiah 62:1-5; Acts 13:16-17,22-25; Matthew 1:1-25

*Reflection:* People use special names when referring to those for whom they deeply care. And in this way they signal a relationship of concern. Husbands create special names for their wives, and wives do the same for their husbands. Friends make up names for each other. Members of a team bestow a special name on a player. Usually, the name refers to a characteristic of the person, something the person has done, or a shortened form of the first or last name.

God, likewise, has special names for people because of his relationship with them. He calls Israel "My Delight' and "Espoused," according to the prophet Isaiah. God is a husband and his people are his wife. Much like a young man marries a virgin, so God chooses a virgin people to be his "delight." Much like a bridegroom rejoices in his bride, God rejoices in his bridal people and calls them his "espoused."

Today the same comparison can be made between God and his Church. He "delights" in his Church, the People of God. He rejoices in them, calling them his "espoused."

The same is true for all of us, especially those who are married. Even though human marriage relationships can falter and break apart, God never abandons the married. He never "forsakes" or leaves them "desolate."

*Meditation:* What special names do you have for others? What special names do others have for you?

*Prayer:* Lord God, in the past you married a people and rejoiced in them. You named them "My Delight" and "Espoused." From this people you brought forth the bridegroom, Jesus Christ, in whom you were well pleased. Do not forsake us or leave us desolate, but send the bridegroom, Jesus, in glory, for he lives and reigns with you and the Holy Spirit, one God, for ever and ever. Amen.

## December 25
## SOLEMNITY OF CHRISTMAS
## Night Into Day
## (Midnight)

The people who walked in darkness
  have seen a great light;
Upon those who dwelt in the land of gloom
  a light has shone.

(Isaiah 9:1)

*Scripture:* Isaiah 9:1-6; Titus 2:11-14; Luke 2:1-14

*Reflection:* People need to learn that they usually must walk through the darkness to get to the light. Many try to walk around the darkness or try to avoid it entirely because they think that darkness is unholy or evil. (For such people, only the light is holy.)

However, those who reflect on past experiences quickly discover that the light is found only after walking through the darkness. If a major decision has to be made concerning a move, a job, a purchase, or surgery, they must walk through the darkness of evaluating the best choice before the light of a final decision is reached. If they experience periods of depression due to loss of a job, money, a death in the family, whatever, they must walk through the depressing darkness if new light is ever to be found.

We have to live through the darkness of pots boiling over, children getting sick, snowstorms, ice storms, floods, tornadoes before the light of the sun shines again. All darkness, all gloom, must be walked through before the light is found. We all walk in darkness before discovering a great light. Each one of us knows the land of gloom before the light shines.

*Meditation:* What was your most recent experience of darkness which was followed by light?

*Prayer:* God of light and darkness, you make holy the night and the day. You remove the yokes of decisions from our shoulders and break the bonds of depression that tie us down. We rejoice in the birth of your Son, Jesus the Christ, the One given to us, the Wonder-Counselor, the God-Hero, the Father-Forever, the Prince of Peace. In your zeal send him to us in glory. He is Lord for ever and ever. Amen.

# SOLEMNITY OF CHRISTMAS
## Called by Name
### (Dawn)

They shall be called the holy people,
   the redeemed of the LORD,
And you shall be called "Frequented,"
   a city that is not forsaken.
                              (Isaiah 62:12)

*Scripture:* Isaiah 62:11-12; Titus 3:4-7; Luke 2:15-20

*Reflection:* People with long names like Benjamin, Bernard, Michael, Catherine, and Veronica are frequently asked what name they prefer. Do they prefer the use of the long form of their names or a shortened version like Ben, Bernie, Mike, Cathy, or Ronnie? People have a right to be called by the name of their choice.

God calls people by generic names, however. One name he uses is "holy people." Holiness is the degree of a person's relationship with God; it presupposes a relationship with him. A "holy people," then, is a people who are like God.

Another name God uses is "redeemed." To be redeemed is to be brought back, rescued, purchased, and set free. This is what God means when he calls people "redeemed."

Isaiah records that God calls people "frequented." He visits people, lives with them, makes a dwelling with them, sets up a tent with them in their camp, builds a home in their community. People who are called "frequented" recognize God's presence with them always.

The Savior, Jesus, bore all these names in his flesh. As a holy person, he showed holiness to others. As a redeemer, he set people free for God. As a frequenter, he lived always with people.

God continues to call all of us by those generic names of "holy," "redeemed," and "frequented." He waits for us to respond to the call. This means that we must recognize the name that God has bestowed upon us.

*Meditation:* When did you last experience being called a holy person or a redeeming individual or a frequenting one?

*Prayer:* Lord God, you proclaim to the ends of the earth that the Savior comes. You have called your people "holy" and "redeemed" as you "frequent" them with your presence. Do not forsake us, as we wait for the coming in glory of the Savior, your Son, our Lord Jesus Christ, who lives and reigns with you and the Holy Spirit, one God, for ever and ever. Amen.

## SOLEMNITY OF CHRISTMAS
### God Is King
### (Daytime)

How beautiful upon the mountains
   are the feet of him who brings glad tidings,
Announcing peace, bearing good news,
   announcing salvation, and saying to Zion,
    "Your God is King!"

                  (Isaiah 52:7)

*Scripture:* Isaiah 52:7-10; Hebrews 1:1-6; John 1:1-18

*Reflection:* Most people do not often think of their feet as being "beautiful." They might have beautiful faces or bodies, or beautiful hands or profiles, but not beautiful feet.

Feet are used for walking, running, kicking, standing, and they get dirty and tired. Feet are thought of as being "down there," near the earth. So, they are taken for granted.

Isaiah proclaims that the messenger who brings good news has happy feet, that is, beautiful feet. Ministry or service to others begins with the feet because they are needed to gain access to others. Once the feet do the walking, then comfort to a patient in a hospital or a nursing home can be given.

Feet enable people to announce peace to others with whom they have fought or argued. They enable individuals to bear the good news of positive reinforcement. They place people in a position to announce salvation to others — whether it is a rescue attempt during a natural disaster, deliverance from enemies, or an invitation to attend a religious gathering.

If we have happy, beautiful feet, we are like Olympic torch-bearers who carry the fire to light the huge torch that signals the beginning of the games. However, unlike Olympic runners, our message is more explosive: "Your God is King!"

Christmas is a celebration for all people. We have been entrusted with this message and mission. Each one of us needs happy feet in order to bear this good news to others.

*Meditation:* What good news are your feet bearing today?

*Prayer:* God, our King, your prophet proclaimed the feet of your messenger to be beautiful in bringing glad tidings, announcing peace and salvation, while proclaiming you to be king. In Jesus, the incarnate "good news," you have restored us, redeemed us, and comforted us. All nations behold your salvation, Lord. Loosen our tongues so that we might break out together in song and praise you for all your works. We ask this through Jesus Christ, your Son, whose coming in glory we await, for he is Lord for ever and ever. Amen.

## December 26
### FEAST OF SAINT STEPHEN
### Faithful Follower

As they were stoning Stephen, he called out, "Lord Jesus, receive my spirit."

(Acts 7:59)

*Scripture:* Acts 6:8-10, 7:54-59; Matthew 10:17-22

*Reflection:* What happens to people who faithfully follow Jesus? They undergo what Jesus underwent — maybe not to the same degree, but God traces the same kind of pattern in their lives that he traced in the life of his only Son.

Stephen is the first New Testament example of what happens to a faithful follower of Jesus. He is called the first martyr, a word which means *witness*. Because his life was patterned after Jesus' life, he was a faithful follower and witness. His suffering and death are portrayed by Luke in the Acts of the Apostles as quite similar to those of Jesus himself.

Just as Jesus' preaching stung the hearts of his listeners, so did Stephen's speech. Jesus saw the sky open as he was baptized and heard the voice of his Father; Stephen saw the sky open as he was being baptized in blood. Just as Luke's Jesus willingly hands over his spirit on the cross, so does Stephen as he breathes his last.

Stephen was crowned with martyrdom; the pattern of his Lord was traced in his own life. He was a faithful follower and witness.

Today we are still called by God to be faithful followers and witnesses. The call may or may not include martyrdom, but the message is the same — to have the pattern of Jesus' life drawn into the outline of our own lives by God. We can do this by spoken and written words, by our actions, decisions, and in many other ways. To be faithful followers of Jesus, our lifestyles must reflect the lifestyle of Jesus.

*Meditation:* What one aspect of your lifestyle identifies you as a faithful follower of Jesus?

*Prayer:* God of martyrs, you are the rock of refuge, a fortress, a stronghold of safety for your people. In the example of Jesus, your servant, you have given us a pattern of holiness. Let your face shine on us. Save us in your kindness. Hide us in the shelter of your presence. Trace the lines of faithfulness in us, as we await your Son's coming in glory. He is Lord for ever and ever. Amen.

## December 27
### FEAST OF SAINT JOHN
### Proclamation

What was from the beginning,
what we have heard,
what we have seen with our eyes,
what we looked upon
and touched with our hands
concerns the Word of life —
for the life was made visible;
we have seen it and testify to it
and proclaim to you the eternal life
that was with the Father and was made visible to us —
what we have seen and heard
we proclaim now to you.

(1 John 1:1-3)

*Scripture:* 1 John 1:1-4; John 20:2-8

*Reflection:* The author of the First Letter of John employs three of the five senses — hearing, seeing, touching — in order to speak of his experiences of the risen Lord. If he could have thought of a way, he probably would have employed the other two senses — tasting and smelling — as well.

The Word of life, Jesus, historically was heard, seen, and touched. Using this historical basis, the author attempts to describe what is beyond history: He relates his own experiences of the risen Lord.

The Incarnation, the becoming-flesh of the invisible God, who is from the beginning, was a great event. But a far more important event is the continuing incarnation of the same God today. This incarnation continues in the flesh of people who form the living body of Christ, the Church.

When people hear the word proclaimed or read from the Bible and begin to live it, they have incarnated it. When people see others in distress — the poor, the helpless, the persecuted — and lend a hand or a few dollars, incarnation has happened again. When they touch others out of love, comfort, sympathy, empathy, or understanding, they make the Word of life visible again. These types of incarnation are not like the one-time-only, historical event of Jesus' Incarnation; these are incarnations of the risen Lord; these transcend history and time.

The spoken word — unrecorded by mechanical means — disappears as quickly as the syllables which form it are pronounced. But they can still be seen and touched (and tasted and smelled) through human flesh.

This is what John proclaims. As an apostle, he was one who was sent forth. As an Evangelist, he announced good news. What John saw, touched, and heard, he made incarnate — in his own flesh. Today we members of the Body of Christ, the Church, must do the same.

*Meditation:* When have you most recently felt the Word of life become incarnate?

*Prayer:* Eternal Father, your invisible Word, Jesus, was present with you from the beginning, but in the glory of the Incarnation he became visible to us. May we be attentive to the words we hear, may we look upon your beauty in all of your creation that we see, may we touch your presence in your people. Make our joy complete, and give us fellowship with you, your Holy Spirit, and your risen Son, Jesus Christ, whose coming in glory we await. He is Lord for ever and ever. Amen.

# December 28
## FEAST OF THE HOLY INNOCENTS
### Darkness and Light

Now this is the message that we have heard from him and proclaim to you: God is light, and in him there is no darkness at all.

(1 John 1:5)

*Scripture:* 1 John 1:5–2:2; Matthew 2:13-18

*Reflection:* The author of the First Letter of John establishes a duality of light and darkness. Light is good because God is light. Darkness is bad because in God there is no darkness. This duality, however, may sometimes reverse roles.

Darkness may be good. Friends often share their specialness or their "secrets" while spending time together on a dark night. Counseling takes place in a semi-lit room. A closeness is felt by people when they gather around a candle set in the middle of a darkened room. Married couples usually make love in the dark of their bedroom, which means that new life is conceived in the dark.

Light may be bad. Light inhibits sharing on a deeper level. Light reveals too much during counseling. Closeness, lovemaking, and conception are not for the broad daylight.

Both light and darkness are good as well as bad. Much depends on the circumstances and the perception of those involved in them. Some can see death as darkness, while others see it as light.

The death of the Holy Innocents, woven by Matthew and based on the death of the children slaughtered by Pharaoh when Moses escaped death, is one of light and darkness. The death of children is certainly darkness. However, the death of children is also light. The children are witnesses, martyrs for two special children: One who would deliver people from the darkness of Egyptian slavery during the night, and the other who would deliver from the darkness of the slavery to sin during an eclipse on a cross. Both of these leaders, Moses and Jesus, brought light to people through darkness. Both the light and the darkness were good and bad.

As followers of Christ, we must dedicate our lives to the task of changing darkness to light.

*Meditation:* Where have you most recently experienced God in the light and in the darkness?

*Prayer:* God of darkness and light, in the night you whispered your word of escape to Moses, and he led your Chosen People from the gloom of Egyptian slavery to the brightness of freedom and the

Promised Land. Likewise, in the night your eternal Word, Jesus, was born to lead all people from the dreariness of sin to the glory of being your sons and daughters. Help us to bear witness to your Christ and follow in his footsteps throughout our nights and our days, as we await his coming in glory. We ask this through the same Christ our Lord. Amen.

## December 29
## True Christians

This is the way we may know that we are in union with him: whoever claims to abide in him ought to live [just] as he lived.

(1 John 2:5-6)

*Scripture:* 1 John 2:3-11; Luke 2:22-35

*Reflection:* On most grade school and high school report cards there is a place for the teacher to give an evaluation of a student's conduct. Conduct is synonymous with behavior; it describes the way people act and indicates their lifestyle.

"Christians" are persons who act like Christ. They demonstrate by their lifestyle that they are followers of Jesus. According to the First Letter of John, the test of being united with Jesus is living as Jesus lived.

All behavior flows from either love or lack of it. People whose lifestyle flows out of love will ask: "Would Jesus do this?" If their lifestyle is not based on love, they ask: "What's in it for me?"

Every day we are confronted with the possibility of conducting ourselves as Jesus would. We prove ourselves true Christians when we follow him despite the prevalent peer pressure and the beguiling bad example of those who insist on ''being like everyone else.'' At work where permanently borrowing a few items is tolerated by most of the employees and the management, as followers of Jesus we must confront stealing. At play when stretching the truth might be understood as part of the daily banter, we must deal with gossip. In homes where children become consumers at an early age — constantly wanting this or that — those of us who are Christian parents must reconsider our attitude toward the poor. The way that we conduct ourselves under these circumstances demonstrates whether or not we are authentic Christians.

*Meditation:* What grade do you give yourself for daily Christian conduct? What one area of your daily life do you need to reform?

*Prayer:* God of truth, through the birth, death, and Resurrection of Jesus you have revealed your love for all people. You have given us your word of love and commanded that we conduct our lives according to it. Make your love perfect in us. Keep us in union with your Son, and help us to follow him faithfully, as we wait for his coming in glory. He is Lord for ever and ever. Amen.

## December 30
## Communication

I am writing to you, children . . . I am writing to you, fathers . . . I am writing to you, young men. . . .

(1 John 2:12-13)

*Scripture:* 1 John 2:12-17; Luke 2:36-40

*Reflection:* There are different ways of communicating with other people. The author of the First Letter of John chose to write a letter.

Another form of communication is by way of the television. Commercials communicate directly with the viewer. Also, a person may personally communicate with one person or a whole group of people. In all cases, a message is relayed or delivered.

God chose to communicate with the whole world through the person of Jesus, his only-begotten Son. The message delivered, according to John, was that sins are forgiven by the one who has existed from the beginning. It was a simple message addressed to the whole world. However, it still has not been fully heard. Are we perhaps among those who have not heard it?

*Meditation:* What message has God most recently communicated to you?

*Prayer:* God, you communicated with the world through your incarnate message, Jesus, your Son. He is your letter of love to us. Help us to be receptive to the good news he brings and to share his glad tidings with all we meet. We ask this through the same Jesus Christ, whose coming in glory we await. He is Lord for ever and ever. Amen.

## December 31
## Final Hour

Children, it is the last hour. . . .
(1 John 2:18)

*Scripture:* 1 John 2:18-21; John 1:1-18

*Reflection:* There is a last hour or a final minute for everything in this world. Every day there is the last hour before midnight. This final hour is celebrated in a special way today, New Year's Eve. At the end of the world, there will be a last hour. Before people die, they will have a final hour. When decisions must be made quickly, those who make them have but the last moments of a final hour to make them. Before the Second Coming of Jesus, the world will have a final hour.

Every day presents multiple final hours in all shapes and forms. The last hour designates that one thing is about to end and something new is about to begin. Final hours teach people that all things, except God, are mortal. All things have a final hour. So last hours prepare Christians over and over again for ends and beginnings in their lives.

There is a promise from God. This promise was demonstrated in

Jesus. During our final hour, which is an end and also a beginning, God promises to be with us. God will never abandon us. All that we can do is to face the final hour and to put our trust in God.

*Meditation:* What was your most recent experience of a last or final hour?

*Prayer:* God of the last hour, in the beginning your Word, Jesus Christ, was with you. Through him all things came into being. In time your Word became flesh and made his dwelling among us. He is the life for the light of all. May we, who believe in his name, we, who have been begotten by you, Father, always be your faithful children, as we await the final hour of the Word's Second Coming. Enable us to see his glory, the glory of an only Son coming from you and filled with the enduring love of your Spirit, who with you and the Son are one God, for ever and ever. Amen.

# FEAST OF THE HOLY FAMILY
## Mutual Respect

The LORD sets a father in honor over his children;
  a mother's authority he confirms over her sons.
He who honors his father atones for sins;
  he stores up riches who reveres his mother.
He who honors his father is gladdened by children,
  and when he prays he is heard.

He who reveres his father will live a long life;
he obeys the LORD who brings comfort to his
mother.

(Sirach 3:2-6)

*Scripture:* Sirach 3:2-6,12-14; Colossians 3:12-21; Matthew 2:13-15,19-23 (A); Luke 2:22-40 or 2:22, 39-40 (B); Luke 2:41-52 (C)

*Reflection:* The author of the Book of Sirach, Jesus, son of Eleazar, son of Sirach (50:27), uses many words to indicate honor, authority, reverence, obedience, and comfort. These words are applied to fathers and mothers. However, they can be applied to the whole family — father, mother, children, brothers, and sisters.

Every person is created in the image and likeness of God. Each one is a reflection of the presence of God in history. Therefore, to respect, to honor, or revere another is to respect, to honor, and to revere the Creator of all. Every human being should show reverence to every other person.

All too often this point is overlooked. We are all equal in human dignity, and this is the bottom line. What separates us, one from another? Income, origins, work — all these and a host of other things have come about through the actions of human beings. While we do not have to be equal in personal gifts or income or work, we are equal in human dignity. Each of us owes respect to every member of our family. We owe respect to every person on earth, no matter what distance separates us — for the earth is a global family.

*Meditation:* When did you last encounter respect because you were a human being worthy of respect? When did you last show respect for another because he or she was a human being worthy of respect?

*Prayer:* Lord God, you have created all people in your image and endowed them with equal human dignity. Set fathers in honor over their children; confirm the authority of mothers over their sons and daughters. Give children the respect and guidance of their parents. May all people respect each other and share in the new life you promise, when your Son, Jesus, will come in glory. He is Lord for ever and ever. Amen.

# January 1
## SOLEMNITY OF MARY, MOTHER OF GOD
### Mary's Name

The Lord said to Moses: " . . . This is how you shall bless the Israelites. Say to them:
The LORD bless you and keep you!
The LORD let his face shine upon you, and be gracious to
    you!
The LORD look upon you kindly and give you peace!
So shall they invoke my name upon the Israelites, and I will
    bless them."

(Numbers 6:22-27)

*Scripture:* Numbers 6:22-27; Galatians 4:4-7; Luke 2:16-21

*Reflection:* Every person has an official name, the one recorded on his or her birth certificate. Often people prefer to be known by shortened versions of their original names. They may have names which were received during high school, referring, for example, to a particular accomplishment in a sports event. Professional sports players have special names. Actors have stage names.

People prefer to name everything, including mountains and their ranges, oceans and their seas, continents and their countries, countries and their states, states and their counties, as well as trees, houses, office buildings, whatever. In effect, it is difficult to imagine something without its proper name.

To be able to call persons by their special names or to name an object gives people control over the individual or the thing. To demonstrate this, shout out someone's name while in a crowd of people, and watch heads turn toward the source of the call.

Names designate status. Names describe. They are pronounced with honor. Not to know an individual's name can be devastating. It is difficult to talk about anyone or anything without knowing his, her, its name.

God gave Moses and Aaron this ability — to call upon him to bless his people. God gave Moses and Aaron his name. Out of love, he risks giving this control to Moses and Aaron. The divine name, however, is to be used only to bless the Israelites, to remind them of their special status, to remind them of God's enduring love and care for them.

Mary, the Mother of Jesus, has many names. Today we refer to her as the Mother of God. She is called the Mother of God because she gave birth to Jesus, who was true man and true God. However, she has many other titles, among them the Virgin, Our Lady, the Queen. These names for Mary describe her in various ways. We use all of these names to honor her.

*Meditation:* How have you most recently used God's name to ask for a blessing or to bless another?

*Prayer:* Lord, you bless us and keep us, you shine your face upon us, and you are gracious to us. As we invoke your name, look upon us kindly and give us peace. May our honor of Mary, the Mother of your Son, give you praise, as we await his coming in glory. He lives with you, Father, and your Holy Spirit, one God, for ever and ever. Amen.

## January 2
## Hearing God's Word

Let what you heard from the beginning remain in you. If what you heard from the beginning remains in you, then you will remain in the Son and in the Father.

(1 John 2:24)

*Scripture:* 1 John 2:22-28; John 1:19-28

*Reflection:* People hear a multitude of sounds every day. They listen to people talking to them; they hear the sound of radios, televisions, and stereos; they are subject to the roar of trucks, cars, and trains; and — it is hoped — they hearken to the words of Scripture when it is proclaimed to them. If what is heard is worthwhile, it should remain in the heart.

If the Word of God truly remains in our hearts, we are united to the Son and the Father. If the Word is in the heart, we become fully alive. All other sounds during a day vie for attention; some get heard, but these are not the pure sounds of God's Word. Sometimes these other sounds can deceive. Only the Word, what was heard from the beginning, should remain in our hearts.

*Meditation:* In your heart, what remains of the Word of God?

*Prayer:* Eternal God, you gave the Torah to Moses to be shared with his descendants forever. In Jesus, your only begotten Son, you spoke your Word in human flesh. Help us to clearly hear his teaching that it might remain in our hearts, so that when he reveals himself in glory we may be fully confident and not retreat in shame at his coming. He is Lord for ever and ever. Amen.

# January 3
# Children of God

See what love the Father has bestowed on us that we may be called the children of God. Yet so we are. . . . We are God's children now; what we shall be has not yet been revealed. We do know that when it is revealed we shall be like him, for we shall see him as he is.

(1 John 3:1-2)

*Scripture:* 1 John 2:29–3:6; John 1:29-34

*Reflection:* People live in three tenses: past, present, and future. The past refers to what is always moving away from the present. The present refers to that which lasts but a mini-second. The future is that which is always moving to the present and quickly passing to the past.

Now, in the present, all people are God's children. They are sons and daughters of God, brothers and sisters of each other. No particular person is responsible for this; it came about solely from the generous and awesome love of God.

In the past, God loved a particular clan of people, the Israelites, and made them his special, chosen possession. But God desired all people; so now, in the present, all are his children.

What of the future? No one knows. No one can know. The most that we can say is that people will be like God and see God as God is. Only one point is clear, and this is based on reliable evidence from the past and God's demonstration of his love for us along with what is known in the present: We can only trust that the future will be glorious. The future is sure to come, and we will share in the glory of God.

*Meditation:* In what way(s) did you experience God's love in the past? In what way(s) do you experience God's love in the present? In what way(s) do you hope to experience God's love in the future?

*Prayer:* Eternal God, past, present, and future are gifts to your people. In the past you have revealed your love by choosing a people and making them your own. Through Jesus, your Son, you have made all people your sons and daughters. As we await the future coming of Jesus in glory, make us holy. We ask this through the same Jesus Christ, who is Lord for ever and ever. Amen.

# January 4
## Truly Holy

Children, let no one deceive you. The person who acts in righteousness is righteous, just as he [Jesus] is righteous. Whoever sins belongs to the devil, because the devil has sinned from the beginning.

(1 John 3:7-8)

*Scripture:* 1 John 3:7-10; John 1:35-42

*Reflection:* Deceit comes in many forms. Sometimes deceit is called a "little white lie," and it is used as a means of self-protection. Major swindling or stealing is a form of deceit designed to protect a lifestyle or a position.

Advertising can be deceitful, as it enumerates, for example, the items a person needs in order to stay young and beautiful without wrinkles or gray hair. Some persons can be deceived by a false sense of self-worth; they *need* to be part of the "right crowd"; they have to be seen in all the *right* places and wear the *latest* clothes. In religion, deceit is named *hypocrisy*. It is easy to deceive and be deceived in this arena.

Holiness, the key to religion, is not necessarily outwardly demonstrated by pietistic acts such as perfectly folded hands, kneeling on hard floors, or lighting candles at every shrine. Holiness is bound up with the degree of a person's relationship with God; this becomes the motivation for everything that is done or not done.

Deceivers are sinners who rely on themselves for everything.

They may be involved in religion; but they do so only to make themselves look good in the eyes of others. The sad part about deceivers is that they most often deceive themselves. Deceivers often "do in" themselves.

If we are authentically holy, we cannot deceive or be deceived. It is not that we do not sin but, rather, that we rely on the forgiveness of God to restore us to the right relationship with him.

*Meditation:* What most recent action or behavior of yours was done out of authentic holiness? out of deceit?

*Prayer:* All-holy God, authentic holiness is begotten through our relationship with you. Continue to draw us closer to yourself that we may be your children in name and in deed as we wait for the coming in glory of Jesus, your Son, who lives and reigns with you and the Holy Spirit, one God, for ever and ever. Amen.

## January 5
## Love One Another

We should love one another. . . . Children, let us love not in word or speech but in deed and truth.

(1 John 3:11,18)

*Scripture:* 1 John 3:11-21; John 1:43-51

*Reflection:* A deed consists of some kind of action; a good one demonstrates love for all. God belongs to all people. All people are equal in human dignity. Love fosters, supports, human dignity, and love urges people to insure it for every man, woman, and child.

Truth is authenticity. Those who love in truth truly love. Their love is not a mask; it flows from the depths of their hearts.

Some people talk a lot about the needs of others, but they never do anything to meet those needs. They criticize previous programs, censure those who staff the programs, and pass judgment on everything that has been done. Those who really love answer the needs of others with deeds of their own. They love in deed and in truth.

If our conscience does not charge us with anything, if there are no twinges of guilt, we can be sure that God is with us, and we are doing and loving in deed and truth and not just talking about it.

*Meditation:* What was your most recent experience of loving in deed and in truth?

*Prayer:* God of love, in the example of Jesus, your Son, we have come to understand love, for he laid down his life for us. Move us to be willing to lay down our lives for our brothers and sisters. Open our eyes to see those in need and enable us to love in deed and in truth. Keep our consciences tuned to your will as we wait in joyful hope for the coming in glory of Jesus, who is Lord for ever and ever. Amen.

# January 6
## Three Testifiers

This is the one who came through water and blood, Jesus Christ, not by water alone, but by water and blood. The Spirit is the one that testifies, and the Spirit is truth. So there are three that testify, the Spirit, the water, and the blood, and the three are of one accord.

(1 John 5:6-8)

*Scripture:* 1 John 5:5-13; Mark 1:7-11

*Reflection:* To testify means to bear witness to the truth. There are three that testify to Jesus as the Son of God.

The first is water. Water was present from the beginning; it represents power. God, however, subdues its power by confining it to the oceans and the seas. The people of Israel crossed through the water of the Sea of Reeds and stepped across the Jordan River to enter the land of promise.

At Jesus' baptism in the Jordan, the voice of God was heard proclaiming Jesus to be the eternal Son. At Cana, water became wine. And on the cross, water and blood flowed from the side of Christ.

The second testifier is blood. Human flesh courses with numerous streams of blood, which carry nourishment to all the cells of the body. Blood was used in the covenant-making ceremony between God and the people: Moses took blood and sprinkled the people and the altar. From the side of Christ, blood flowed forth as he hung his head in death. And before his death, Jesus sweat blood in the Garden.

The Spirit is the third witness. The Spirit was present at creation, hovering over the water. It took the form of a dove at Jesus' baptism and it raised the crucified Lord from the dead. The Spirit broods over wine and changes it into the blood of Christ.

What more is needed to convince us of the Incarnation? These three continue, all around the world, to remind us of what we believe and celebrate. Water continues to pour forth from faucets, streams, rivers, lakes, and oceans. Blood continues to be given away as the ''gift of life'' to blood banks. And in every breath, every whisper of wind, every storm, the presence of the Spirit is made known.

*Meditation:* When was the last time that you were made aware of or experienced the incarnation of Jesus in water, blood, or Spirit?

*Prayer:* God of Jesus, you testified to your Son's incarnation in water, blood, and your Spirit. You have given us eternal life; may we always realize that we possess this life as we grow in belief in the name of the Son of God, whose coming in glory we await. We ask this of you, Father, through Jesus Christ, our Lord, who lives and reigns with you and the Holy Spirit, one God, for ever and ever. Amen.

# January 7
# False Gods

Children, be on your guard against idols.
(1 John 5:21)

*Scripture:* 1 John 5:14-21; John 2:1-12

*Reflection:* Not only is there a commandment which prohibits the worship of idols, but most of the Old Testament is a warning to the Israelites to be sure that they do not adore false gods. The injunction against false gods was aimed at the pagan gods of wood, stone, and metal made by the various peoples with whom the Chosen People came in contact.

Today the prohibition against worshiping false gods as understood in this primitive sense seems almost ridiculous to people of the technological era. However, there might be other ways of looking at false gods. Sometimes relationships, children, money, a job situation, and even self can become a god that a person worships.

It is easy to create such idols, focusing on these rather than concentrating on the one, true God. Idols can get as much in the way today as they did in the past, coming between God and people.

Idols are more appealing because they are tangible in contrast to the God who cannot be physically touched. Idols can be seen in contrast to the God who is invisible. Awards of honor can be given to an idol and rewards received from it, while God is often silent.

We should remember, of course, that idols are the work of

human hands: Idols are made by people. If the time spent on creating idols was used to develop our relationship with God, not only would that relationship flourish but we would get all we need and more besides.

*Meditation:* What idol interferes with your relationship with God?

*Prayer:* One God, we are confident that you hear us whenever we petition you according to your will. Remove all idols that interfere with our relationship with you. Help us to follow in the footsteps of Jesus, your Son, who has given us the gift of discernment to recognize you, who are the true God and eternal life. We ask this through Jesus Christ, whose coming in glory we await. He is Lord for ever and ever. Amen.


# SOLEMNITY OF THE EPIPHANY
## God's Glory Manifested


Rise up in splendor! Your light has come,
the glory of the Lord shines upon you.
See, darkness covers the earth,
and thick clouds cover the peoples;
But upon you the LORD shines,
and over you appears his glory.

(Isaiah 60:1-2)


*Scripture:* Isaiah 60:1-6; Ephesians 3:2-3,5-6; Matthew 2:1-12

*Reflection:* The word *epiphany* means *manifestation, revelation, showing forth*. An epiphany is like a flash of light after a long period of darkness. It is a streak of light through a dark, cloudy sky.

Most people have experienced cloudy, gloomy, dark days in their lives — times when they found it difficult to crawl out of bed and get the morning started. The clouds get worse as the day progresses. And when night finally falls, decisions made in haste and ignorance come back to haunt the decision-makers.

In the midst of such thick clouds, sooner or later a light breaks through. Something positive about a new day comes to mind; that feeling of being tired — caused by the burden of work — comes to a momentary pause, and life begins to shine again. A new light of learning streaks into life, which hopefully will be remembered.

There are always dark clouds gathering in our lives. Such darkness helps us to appreciate the streaks of light. Every time that light flashes through the darkness, God is present. An epiphany is taking place again!

*Meditation:* What was your most recent experience of dark clouds followed by the light of God's presence?

*Prayer:* God of glory, in the darkness you offer us light and part the thick clouds with your shining radiance. You gather us to yourself as a mother holds her child in her loving arms. Make our hearts throb and overflow in your presence. May the riches of our lives be emptied out before you in praise as we await the Second Coming in glory of your Son, our Lord Jesus Christ, who lives and reigns with you and the Holy Spirit, one God, for ever and ever. Amen.

# Monday After Epiphany
## Testing of Spirits

Beloved, do not trust every spirit but test the spirits to see whether they belong to God.

(1 John 4:1)

*Scripture:* 1 John 3:22–4:6; Matthew 4:12-17,23-25

*Reflection:* The meaning of the word *spirit* (spelled with a lower case "s") is not drink (as in whiskey) nor *Spirit* (spelled with an upper case "S") as in Holy Spirit. The meaning of "spirit" might better be rendered as *attitude*.

There is a definite attitude among the fans gathered in a stadium or an arena for a sports event. Most of those there get caught up in the game, caught up in the spirit. Likewise, a specific attitude exists among the players on a team no matter whether they are on a field, on a court, or on a rink. Their playing together exemplifies a particular spirit.

Families can possess the spirit of cooperation. Co-workers can share the burden of the job by assuming a specific attitude or spirit. In a school there is not only a school spirit but also each class might be said to have "class spirit," where all get behind a project and pull together. People in specific neighborhoods work together to keep their geographical area clean, to watch each other's homes when some are away, and to protect each other's children. These are examples of the true meaning of spirit.

There are other kinds of spirit, however. Some people seek the spirit of revenge; they want to get even when they are hurt physically or emotionally. Guilt or shame triggers the spirit of withdrawal of one person from a group. A spirit of destruction fosters the desecration of property and reputations. Some persons may be scared to ''speak out'' due to the spirit of mistrust or fear. A spirit of ''me first'' often means that a person *must* be ''number one'' and has no concern for others.

All our spirits or attitudes need to be tested. The test is simple: An authentic spirit from God is one that asks if the dignity of every human person is being respected. True spirits or attitudes uphold human dignity as manifested in human flesh. By becoming human, Jesus gave human flesh greater dignity than it already had from the first day that it was created. When any spirit or attitude does not acknowledge this, it cannot be from God.

*Meditation:* Name two spirits that belong to God and two that do not that you have most recently experienced.

*Prayer:* God of truth, whatever we ask we receive from your hands. You have raised us up in dignity and poured out your goodness on us through the Incarnation of Jesus, your Son. Help us to keep your commandments and to do what is pleasing in your sight as we await the Second Coming of him who is Lord for ever and ever. Amen.

# Tuesday After Epiphany
## God Is Love

God is love. In this way the love of God was revealed to us: God sent his only Son into the world so that we might have life through him. In this is love: not that we have loved God, but that he loved us and sent his Son as expiation for our sins.

(1 John 4:8-10)

*Scripture:* 1 John 4:7-10; Mark 6:34-44

*Reflection:* Any form of the verb *to be* means *equal*. Used in a sentence, this verb takes a predicate nominative for its object because it is really a subject. Therefore, to say that "God is love" is to say that God equals love.

Love, although a much misunderstood word, is experienced in all human relationships. Parents love their children, and children love their parents. Siblings display their love for their brothers and sisters. For teenagers, love usually means infatuation. Adult love is shared in freedom and trust. Mature love ages with wrinkles and memories and fallibility. These experiences are but a human taste of God, who is love.

So great, so powerful, and so overwhelming is God's love that he wanted to share this love with his creatures. God therefore sent his Son into the world to become flesh. This human and divine life line that coursed through Jesus was offered by God for his people to share.

This first movement of love was made by God much as we all make a move to meet and get to know others in the hope of loving them. God loves us first and asks us to enter into the experience of love. He invites us to get caught up in the love of the One who is love. God *equals* the purest form of love.

*Meditation:* Besides Jesus, who represents incarnate love for you? How?

*Prayer:* God of love, you revealed yourself in our midst by sending your only Son, Jesus, into the world as an offering for our sins that we might have life through him. Enable us to reach out in love to all of our brothers and sisters and to share with them the joy of the Incarnation of Jesus, whose coming in glory we await. He is Lord for ever and ever. Amen.

## Wednesday After Epiphany
## Love Drives Out Fear

There is no fear in love, but perfect love drives out fear. . . .
(1 John 4:18)

*Scripture:* 1 John 4:11-18; Mark 6:45-52

*Reflection:* Fear takes many forms, that is, it has many synonyms. Terror is a form of fear. Trauma is a form of fear. Being afraid is a form of fear.

The state of loneliness can be extremely fearful for some people. People fear others who have the power to conquer them. On planes and ships terrorists can cause fear. There is even psychological fear of what others will think. When new situations, which have never been confronted before, develop at work or in relationships, people immediately fear.

Fear emotionally paralyzes people. It stifles creativity and numbs the emotions.

Where there is love, however, there is no room for fear. Perfect love casts out all fear. Love matures in a climate of trust. Where there is trust, there cannot be fear; both trust and fear cannot coexist. It is impossible to fear and trust simultaneously.

People who fear punishment from God or see disasters — natural and human-made — as punishment from God do not really love God. People who are willing to do God's will because they trust God have no fear.

Love frees people from fear. Husbands and wives who have built solid, authentic love relationships on trust cannot possibly fear each other. Friends who share their inner selves (beings) with one another because of their trust in one another cannot know fear.

When we remove our masks and can stand before another or God as we would stand before a mirror and see ourselves as we truly are, there is no fear. When we can look at ourselves in the trust and love of God, admitting both the good and the bad within us, there is no fear. Love drives out fear.

*Meditation:* Do you love God out of fear, or do you love God out of trust?

*Prayer:* Loving God, no one has ever seen you, yet we know that when we love one another you dwell in us and your love is brought to perfection in us. We have come to believe that you are love, and we who abide in love abide in you and you in us. Cast out all our fear and make your love perfect in us as we wait for the coming in glory of your only-begotten Son, Jesus Christ, who lives and reigns with you and the Holy Spirit in perfect love, one God, for ever and ever. Amen.

## Thursday After Epiphany
### Love of God and Neighbor

If anyone says, "I love God," but hates his brother, he is a liar; for whoever does not love a brother whom he has seen cannot love God whom he has not seen."

(1 John 4:20)

*Scripture:* 1 John 4:19–5:4; Luke 4:14-22

*Reflection:* To be able to see is a wonderful gift from God. Those who are physically blind learn to "see" others through the sense of touch. What people see is considered by most to be reality (although seeing can sometimes be illusory). A love relationship is best fostered between a husband and a wife or a friend and a friend or a child and a parent in the visible or physical presence of the other. It is not impossible to carry on a long-distance love relationship through the use of photographs, letters, telephone calls, and tapes, but it can become difficult at times. There is something positive and important to the visible presence of another; this makes it easier to love another.

God sees people and loves them. He makes the first move to get to know people and to love them. He initiates a relationship of love with people.

God, of course, cannot be seen. This makes a return of love on the part of people difficult but not impossible. So, to help remedy the situation, God makes human love between two persons a mirror of God's love for all people. When people love each other who can be seen, they are in effect loving God, who cannot be seen. When people love God who cannot be seen, they are in effect loving others who can be seen.

God's greatest vision of love, of course, is Jesus, who is the incarnate presence of love. The visible Jesus reflected the love of the invisible God.

For this reason when we say we love God, we must also love our brothers and sisters. This is why we make ourselves liars when we say our love is fixed on God while at the same time we have hatred for our brothers and sisters.

*Meditation:* Who reflects visibly for you the love of the God whom you cannot see?

*Prayer:* Invisible God, you have first loved us and made visible your love in the Incarnation of Jesus, your only-begotten Son. Through the love we have for the brothers and sisters whom we can see, enable us to love you, whom we cannot see. We ask this through our Lord Jesus Christ, whose Second Coming in glory we await; he lives and reigns with you, Father, and the Holy Spirit in invisible love, one God, for ever and ever. Amen.

# Friday After Epiphany
## Victors

Who [indeed] is the victor over the world but the one who believes that Jesus is the Son of God.

(1 John 5:5)

*Scripture:* 1 John 5:5-13; Luke 5:12-16

*Reflection:* A victor is one who has conquered. To call someone a victor is to imply a defeat of some kind. When the two top-ranked sports teams battle it out on the field, on the court, or on the rink, the team that wins is the victor. A victory is announced when one corporation either forces another one out of business or buys it out. Even in personal life, individuals can become victors when they overcome fears or phobias or psychological problems. No matter what the victor conquers, the same show of force is necessary.

Is there some other way? The author of the first letter of John believes that there is. The world can be conquered by faith. This is true not only for Christians, but for anyone who believes in God.

How? Faith, authentic conviction, enables a person to suffer all, to abandon all, to be stripped of all — even life — in order to claim the prize of authenticity. Such people are appropriately named witnesses (martyrs) because they give testimony by their steadfastness, their faith. Because of their faith, the world is overcome.

Today, more often than not, steadfastness to the point of death is nonexistent. With the first bit of suffering or inconvenience in the area of faith, people turn to whomever or to whatever it is convenient to believe. This noncommitted stance seems to be the order of the day. People want to "go with the flow."

The real victor, however, looks like the one who is conquered. For us, the real victor looks out on the world from the cross, just like Jesus did. In truth, however, it is those of us who look like we are conquered, defeated, who are the real victors over the world.

*Meditation:* What has been your most recent experience of being a victor over the world?

*Prayer:* God of eternal life, you sent your Son, Jesus, to us through water and blood in order to conquer the world. Make our faith in him strong, give us eternal life, and fill us with the Spirit of truth, as we wait in joyful hope for the coming in glory of him who, with you and the Holy Spirit, live and reign as one God, for ever and ever. Amen.

## Saturday After Epiphany
## Confidence in God

We have this confidence in him, that if we ask anything according to his will, he hears us. And if we know that he hears us in regard to whatever we ask, we know that what we have asked him for is ours.

(1 John 5:14-15)

*Scripture:* 1 John 5:14-21; John 3:22-30

*Reflection:* Confidence is based on faith, which in turn is defined as belief without proof. Personal belief or confidence in God derives from a person's past experiences of God at work in his or her life.

Confidence, according to the author of the First Letter of John, means personal trust in a God who listens to the requests of his creatures. The only qualification is to ask according to God's will. But first the mind of God must be probed in order to discern his will about what is being asked.

If we discern God's will first — by spending a few moments in meditation and contemplation to enhance our already-well-established relationship with the deity — then we can have confidence that whatever is asked for according to God's will will be granted. This is confidence as it was meant to be.

*Meditation:* What was your most recent experience of receiving from God what you asked for after you discerned God's will for you?

*Prayer:* God of trust, you take delight in all of your people who have been begotten of you and who seek your truth. Make strong our confidence in you. Hear us whenever we ask for anything according to your will. Inspire us to know your will that we might be confident in hope as we wait for the coming in glory of your Son, our Lord Jesus Christ, who lives and reigns with you and the Holy Spirit, one God, for ever and ever. Amen.

# FEAST OF THE BAPTISM OF THE LORD
## Victory of Justice

I, the LORD, have called you for the victory of justice,
   I have grasped you by the hand;
I formed you, and set you
   as a covenant of the people,
   a light for the nations,
To open the eyes of the blind,
   to bring out prisoners from confinement,
   and from the dungeon, those who live in darkness.
                         (Isaiah 42:6-7)

*Scripture:* Isaiah 42:1-4,6-7; Acts 10:34-38; Matthew 3:13-17 (A); Mark 1:7-11 (B); Luke 3:15-16,21-22 (C)

*Reflection:* Through the waters of Baptism, every human being has been chosen for, called to, and initiated into the victory of justice. A victory is a triumph, a win. Justice is concern and care for those who lack justice. Traditionally, those on the fringes of society are known as the poor, the widow, and the orphan. Isaiah adds the blind, the imprisoned, and those in dungeons.

Justice has little to do with the American system of jurisprudence; this system is concerned with what is legally fair. Biblical justice is concerned with what is ethical, with what is morally correct.

Through the waters of Baptism, a person is plunged into the mission of justice. Each person becomes a covenant, an incarnation of justice, a sign of justice in the world. The newly baptized person is given a candle to represent that he or she is a light to the nations, a light that shines justice in the midst of racial, economic, and sexual prejudices. The light of justice must, of course, be seen in order to be effective.

The victory of justice can easily be defeated by apathy or by a "me first" attitude. The baptismal mission, however, moves us outward — not inward — as members of a community who strive for the victory of justice for others. The ideal challenge, the ideal victory, is to totally eliminate all need from the face of the earth. Indeed, this would be our victory of justice.

*Meditation:* When was the last time that you participated in the victory of justice?

*Prayer:* God of justice, you chose Jesus, the servant and Son in whom you were pleased, to bring forth justice. On him you put your Spirit so that he could open the eyes of the blind and bring out prisoners from confinement and those who live in darkness from the dungeon. Through the waters of Baptism you have called us to follow in his steps and to work for the victory of justice. Grasp us by the hand and make us a light of justice as we wait for the coming in glory of Jesus, who lives and reigns with you and the Holy Spirit, one God, for ever and ever. Amen.

Because the number of days in the Advent and Christmas seasons varies and because the liturgical calendar for these seasons changes slightly each year, this chart is provided to help you use this book more easily.

First, locate the appropriate date. Second, look across to the column headed by the current year. Third, turn to the page listed.

## ADVENT/CHRISTMAS SEASONS CHART

|  | 1989 | 1990 | 1991 | 1992 | 1993 |
|---|---|---|---|---|---|
| November 28 | – | – | – | – | 17 |
| 29 | – | – | – | 16 | 19 |
| 30 | – | – | – | 19 | 21 |
| December 1 | – | – | 18 | 21 | 22 |
| 2 | – | 17 | 19 | 22 | 23 |
| 3 | 16 | 19 | 21 | 23 | 25 |
| 4 | 19 | 21 | 22 | 25 | 26 |
| 5 | 21 | 22 | 23 | 26 | *31 |
| 6 | 22 | 23 | 25 | 30 | 35 |
| 7 | 23 | 25 | 27 | 35 | 37 |
| 8 | 27 | 27 | 33 | 27 | 27 |
| 9 | 26 | 31 | 35 | 38 | 40 |
| 10 | 30 | 35 | 37 | 40 | 42 |
| 11 | 35 | 37 | 38 | 42 | 43 |
| 12 | 45 | 45 | 45 | 45 | 49 |
| 13 | 38 | 40 | 42 | 48 | 52 |
| 14 | 40 | 42 | 43 | 52 | 54 |
| 15 | 42 | 43 | 51 | 54 | 55 |
| 16 | 43 | 49 | 52 | 55 | 57 |
| 17 | 48 | 61 | 61 | 61 | 61 |
| 18 | 63 | 63 | 63 | 63 | 63 |
| 19 | 71 | 71 | 71 | 71 | 68 |
| 20 | 73 | 73 | 73 | 66 | 73 |

|          |    | 1989 | 1990 | 1991 | 1992 | 1993 |
|----------|----|------|------|------|------|------|
| December | 21 | 75   | 75   | 75   | 75   | 75   |
|          | 22 | 78   | 78   | 69   | 78   | 78   |
|          | 23 | 80   | 68   | 80   | 80   | 80   |
| Morning  | 24 | 66   | 82   | 82   | 82   | 82   |
| Vigil    | 24 | 84   | 84   | 84   | 84   | 84   |
| Midnight | 25 | 85   | 85   | 85   | 85   | 85   |
| Dawn     | 25 | 87   | 87   | 87   | 87   | 87   |
| Daytime  | 25 | 89   | 89   | 89   | 89   | 89   |
|          | 26 | 90   | 90   | 90   | 90   | 99   |
|          | 27 | 92   | 92   | 92   | 99   | 92   |
|          | 28 | 94   | 94   | 94   | 94   | 94   |
|          | 29 | 96   | 96   | 100  | 96   | 96   |
|          | 30 | 98   | 100  | 98   | 98   | 98   |
|          | 31 | 100  | 99   | 99   | 99   | 99   |

|         |    | 1990 | 1991 | 1992 | 1993 | 1994 |
|---------|----|------|------|------|------|------|
| January | 1  | 102  | 102  | 102  | 102  | 102  |
|         | 2  | 104  | 104  | 104  | 104  | 113  |
|         | 3  | 105  | 105  | 105  | 113  | 115  |
|         | 4  | 107  | 107  | 107  | 115  | 117  |
|         | 5  | 108  | 108  | 113  | 117  | 118  |
|         | 6  | 110  | 113  | 115  | 118  | 120  |
|         | 7  | 113  | 115  | 117  | 120  | 122  |
|         | 8  | 125  | 117  | 118  | 122  | 123  |
|         | 9  | –    | 118  | 120  | 123  | 125  |
|         | 10 | –    | 120  | 122  | 125  | –    |
|         | 11 | –    | 122  | 123  | –    | –    |
|         | 12 | –    | 123  | 125  | –    | –    |
|         | 13 | –    | 125  | –    | –    | –    |